# SAVORY SOUPS and STEWS

RODALE'S
New
Classics™

# SAVORY SOUPS and STEWS

## By Anne Egan

RODALE

Cover and Interior Designer: Richard Kershner

Cover and Interior Photos: Rodale Images


Front Cover Recipe: Beef Burgundy (page 79)


**Library of Congress Cataloging-in-Publication Data**

Egan, Anne.

    Savory soups and stews / by Anne Egan.

        p.    cm. — (Rodale's new classics)

    Includes index.

    ISBN 1–57954–286–7 paperback

    1. Soups.  2. Stews.  I. Title.

  TX757. E34  2000

  641.8'13—dc21          00–009100

**Distributed to the book trade by St. Martin's Press**

2  4  6  8  10  9  7  5  3  1  paperback

Visit us on the Web at www.rodalecookbooks.com, or call us toll-free at (800) 848-4735.

WE **INSPIRE** AND **ENABLE** PEOPLE TO IMPROVE
THEIR LIVES AND THE WORLD AROUND THEM

**BEEF AND
BLACK BEAN
CHILI**
Page 76

**SOUTHWEST
SHRIMP
STEW**
Page 95

# Contents

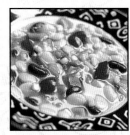

**MINESTRONE**
Page 53

**CREAMY
CHICKEN
CHOWDER**
Page 11

# Introduction

**The most satisfying of comfort foods,** soups and stews are the ideal combination of all good things to eat. Most people can't resist the rich meld of flavors and textures that make up these simmering dishes.

Traditionally, soups and stews have taken hours and even days to prepare. Although this laborious cooking provides rich flavors, many of the time-consuming steps can be eliminated by using readily available products such as prepared broth, cubed meats, seasoning mixes, and canned tomatoes.

In *Rodale's New Classics*, I show you how to make great meals without spending all day in the kitchen. I take traditional, favorite recipes— *the ones you really want to eat*—and make them quick and easy for today's hectic lifestyles. I have done this by using the fastest ingredients and cooking techniques whenever possible. For example, elegant

Bouillabaisse with Herbed Toast (page 90) can be on the table in just 25 minutes.

Cooking can be an enjoyable activity. I find cooking a great stress reliever after a long day, as well as an enjoyable weekend activity with family and friends. Knowing what to cook and how to do so easily is what makes it a fun pastime. So relax and enjoy preparing these family-favorite comfort foods.

## Soup and Stew Basics

Soups and stews have many of the same features. Stews have a thicker sauce that laces chunks of vegetables and meat, poultry, or fish such as my Beef Burgundy (page 79). Soups are a bit more varied. Soups may have a thick or thin broth and may contain meat, poultry, or fish, or just vegetables, like my Ginger Carrot Soup (page 64).

Following are some basic ingredient and cooking tips that pertain to both soups and stews.

**Prepared broths.** Using prepared broths gives immediate flavor to soups and stews. Do beware of the high sodium content. I find that the organic broths contain less sodium and other unnecessary ingredients. Low-sodium versions are also available. Both of these options seem to have more intense meat or vegetable flavor than the full-sodium broths.

**Vegetables.** I call for using fresh vegetables as much as possible in recipes since they impart the greatest flavors. While simmering in a soup or stew, fresh vegetables maintain their texture much better than frozen or canned ones. The exceptions for ease in preparation are frozen peas, corn, and spinach. If time is of the essence, go ahead and substitute frozen vegetables.

**Beans.** Dried beans produce delicious soups but can take a long time to prepare. For this reason, only a few of my recipes use the dried variety. With so many canned bean options on market shelves, a soup or stew prepared with them can be a quick, healthy, and delicious meal. Rinsing the beans eliminates about half of the salt added in the canning process, so be sure to give them a rinse before adding to the pot.

**Meat and poultry.** For the speediest meals, take advantage of the prepared cuts of meat and poultry available. Cubed beef, pork, and lamb save time and energy in the kitchen as do boneless, skinless chicken breast strips. If you buy a large cut of meat or poultry, trim the fat or remove the skin before cooking.

**Fish and shellfish.** With all of the news today touting the health benefits of fish and seafood, soups and stews are a great way to include them in your meals. Feel free to vary the fish in these recipes to include your favorite ones. When preparing finfish, such as salmon, flounder, or cod, be sure to remove the bones and skin before using. Needle-nose pliers work well for removing those stubborn little bones. Mollusks, such as clams and mussels, must be purchased while still alive. Once cooked, they will open to expose the meat. Discard any unopened shells.

**Dairy products.** When adding milk, buttermilk, or sour cream to a soup or stew, do so at the very end of the cooking time. After adding the dairy product, cook just until heated through to prevent curdling.

**Thickeners.** Flour and cornstarch are the most common thickeners for soups and stews. Flour is usually added at the beginning of the cooking time. It is important to cook the flour in hot oil or butter for a few minutes. This can be done either by coating the meat or poultry prior to browning or by sprinkling it on cooked vegetables and cooking for a moment before adding the liquid. Cornstarch is added at the end of the cooking time. Be sure to dissolve it in a bit of cold water or broth before adding to a hot mixture to prevent lumping. Cornstarch needs to boil for a few minutes to thicken properly.

**Flavor enhancers.** You may vary a soup or stew's character simply by changing the seasoning. When selecting a flavor for a recipe, I often choose a few herbs or spices that I think may work nicely and then I smell each one to see how it would add to the dish. Besides herbs and spices, try adding citrus juices and grated peel, prepared mustard, horseradish, wasabi, or other condiments.

**Saucepan.** It is important to use a large enough saucepan when cooking soups and stews. The recipes in this book call for a large saucepan, at least 4 quarts. A soup pot or Dutch oven will also work well.

**Pureeing.** Soups that are pureed have a rich, thick texture. Use a blender, food processor, or handheld immersion blender to puree soups. If none of these are available to you, try a ricer or potato masher. Work carefully when pureeing hot soups. Processing the soup in batches makes the procedure easier and a bit safer.

**Storing.** Most soups and stews can be made ahead and refrigerated for later use. This often improves the flavor. Always cool before storing the soup in a tightly covered container in the refrigerator. Most soups and stews can be refrigerated for up to 3 days before use, but those made with fish and seafood should be used by the next day. I usually make double batches and freeze one for later use. Package as you would for storing in the refrigerator; just be sure that there is at least a half-inch of head space to allow for expansion. Thaw in the refrigerator before reheating in a saucepan over medium-low heat.

Because soups and stews are a wholesome, simple entrée in one pot, incorporate more of them into your meal plans. So easy and delicious, all you will need to balance out a meal is a tossed salad, a loaf of bread and, perhaps, a bottle of fine wine. Enjoy!

*Anne Egan*

# ROBUST POULTRY AND MEAT SOUPS

# Creamy Chicken Chowder

3 cups chicken broth
3 carrots, chopped
2 ribs celery, chopped
1 onion, chopped
1 clove garlic, minced
2 ounces mushrooms, sliced
¼ teaspoon salt
1 teaspoon chopped fresh rosemary
1 pound boneless, skinless chicken breast, cut into ¾" pieces
2 tablespoons butter
3 tablespoons unbleached all-purpose flour
1 cup milk
1 cup fresh or frozen and thawed peas
1 tablespoon chopped fresh parsley
¼ teaspoon freshly ground black pepper

*A puree of favorite vegetables—carrots, celery, onions, and mushrooms—thickens this sensational chowder. Serve with biscuits or bread to make a hearty one-dish meal.*

Combine the broth, carrots, celery, onion, garlic, mushrooms, salt, and rosemary in a large saucepan. Bring to a boil over high heat. Reduce the heat to low, cover, and simmer for 20 minutes, or until the vegetables are tender. Using a slotted spoon, transfer half of the vegetable mixture to a food processor. Process until pureed. Return to the saucepan.

Stir in the chicken and simmer, covered, for 15 minutes, or until the chicken is no longer pink.

Melt the butter in a small saucepan over medium heat. Stir in the flour until smooth. Cook, stirring, for 1 minute. Gradually add the milk and cook, stirring constantly, for 3 minutes, or until thickened. Stir into the chicken mixture. Add the peas, parsley, and pepper. Cook for 5 minutes, or until the mixture is heated through and the peas are tender.

**Makes 4 servings**
*Per serving: 347 calories, 40 g protein, 22 g carbohydrates, 12 g fat, 109 mg cholesterol, 5 g fiber, 775 mg sodium*

# Chicken and Black Bean Soup

2  tablespoons olive oil

1  pound boneless, skinless chicken breasts, cut into ¾" pieces

1  onion, chopped

1  rib celery, chopped

1  red bell pepper, chopped

5½ cups chicken broth

¼  cup Texmati or converted rice

2  bay leaves

1  teaspoon ground cumin

1  teaspoon curry powder

½  teaspoon dried thyme leaves

¼  teaspoon ground allspice

1  can (14½ ounces) black beans, rinsed and drained

1  tablespoon lime juice

¼  cup chopped fresh cilantro

*In this cumin-curry spiced recipe, tasty go-togethers—chicken, rice, and beans—make for a family-pleasing soup. Spice up the presentation by swirling a dollop of sour cream into each serving.*

Heat the oil in a large saucepan over medium-high heat. Add the chicken and cook for 5 minutes, stirring often, until browned. Using a slotted spoon, remove to a bowl. Add the onion, celery, and bell pepper. Cook, stirring occasionally, for 7 minutes, or until the vegetables are tender.

Add the broth, rice, bay leaves, cumin, curry, thyme, allspice, and chicken. Bring to a boil over high heat. Reduce the heat to low, cover, and simmer for 25 minutes, or until the chicken and rice are tender, stirring occasionally.

Add the beans and cook for 5 minutes to heat through. Stir in the lime juice and cilantro.

**Makes 4 servings**

*Per serving: 353 calories, 40 g protein, 29 g carbohydrates, 11 g fat, 88 mg cholesterol, 8 g fiber, 1,081 mg sodium*

# Dilled Chicken Soup with Matzo Balls

2 eggs

½ cup matzo meal

3 tablespoons chopped fresh dill

4 cups chicken broth

1 pound boneless, skinless chicken breasts, cut into ¾" pieces

2 carrots, chopped

1 rib celery, chopped

1 onion, chopped

¼ teaspoon salt

½ teaspoon freshly ground black pepper

*Matzo ball soup is traditionally served at the Passover Seder, but chicken and fresh dill make this dish a treat any time. To serve a crowd, simply double the recipe.*

Using a fork, beat the eggs in a small bowl until frothy. Slowly beat in the matzo meal and 1 tablespoon of the dill. Refrigerate, covered, for at least 10 minutes.

In a large saucepan, bring the broth to a boil over high heat. Add the chicken, carrots, celery, onion, salt, and pepper. Reduce the heat to low, cover, and simmer for 13 minutes.

Meanwhile, shape the matzo mixture into 8 balls. (For each ball, use about 1 tablespoon of the mixture. Dampen your hands with cold water and roll the mixture into a ball between your palms.)

Increase the heat to medium-high and bring the soup to a gentle boil. Drop the matzo balls into the pot. Reduce the heat to low, cover, and simmer for 10 minutes, or until the matzo balls are cooked through. Stir in the remaining 2 tablespoons dill.

**Makes 4 servings**

*Per serving: 295 calories, 39 g protein, 20 g carbohydrates, 7 g fat, 194 mg cholesterol, 3 g fiber, 845 mg sodium*

# Old-Fashioned Chicken-Vegetable Soup

- 2 tablespoons olive oil
- 1 pound boneless, skinless chicken breasts, cut into ¾" pieces
- 2 cloves garlic, minced
- 1 onion, chopped
- 4 cups chicken broth
- ¾ pound green beans, cut into 2" lengths (about 1½ cups)
- 1½ cups fresh or frozen and thawed corn kernels
- 1 red bell pepper, chopped
- 1 rib celery, chopped
- 1 small zucchini, quartered lengthwise and sliced
- 4 sprigs thyme
- ¼ teaspoon salt
- ½ teaspoon freshly ground pepper
- ¼ cup loosely packed celery leaves
- 2 tablespoons chopped fresh parsley

*Not your run-of-the-mill chicken soup. This version sports seven different vegetables and a lively thyme flavor.*

Heat the oil in a large saucepan over medium-high heat. Add the chicken and cook, stirring occasionally, for 10 minutes, or until lightly browned. Add the garlic and onion. Cook, stirring often, for 8 minutes, or until the onion is translucent.

Add the broth, beans, corn, bell pepper, celery, zucchini, thyme, salt, and pepper. Bring to a boil. Reduce the heat to low, cover, and simmer for 10 minutes, or until the beans are tender. Remove and discard the thyme. Stir in the celery leaves and parsley.

**Makes 4 servings**

*Per serving: 342 calories, 39 g protein, 26 g carbohydrates, 11 g fat, 88 mg cholesterol, 7 g fiber, 807 mg sodium*

**COOKING TIP**

When cooking herb sprigs in a soup or stew, tie the sprigs together with kitchen twine for easy removal from the pot.

# Chicken Minestrone

2 tablespoons olive oil

1 large onion, thinly sliced

1 teaspoon poultry seasoning

3 cups chicken broth

2 cups water

1 can (14 ounces) whole tomatoes, chopped

1 pound cooked chicken breast, shredded into large pieces

½ pound green beans, cut into 1" pieces

¼ head small cabbage, coarsely chopped

¾ cup shell pasta

2 teaspoons chopped fresh sage or 1 teaspoon dried

½ teaspoon freshly ground black pepper

¼ teaspoon salt

*No two minestrones are alike. This version features succulent chicken, green cabbage, and pasta shells. Sage and poultry seasoning give the broth an interesting complexity. Round out the meal with focaccia bread fresh from the oven.*

Heat the oil in a large saucepan over medium-high heat. Add the onion and poultry seasoning and cook for 5 minutes. Add the broth, water, and tomatoes (with juice) and bring to a boil. Reduce the heat to low, cover, and simmer for 5 minutes.

Stir in the chicken, green beans, cabbage, pasta, sage, pepper, and salt. Simmer, covered, for 8 minutes, or until the vegetables and pasta are tender.

**Makes 4 servings**

*Per serving: 363 calories, 38 g protein, 26 g carbohydrates, 11 g fat, 87 mg cholesterol, 4 g fiber, 865 mg sodium*

# Sweet Potato and Turkey Soup

- 4 cups chicken broth
- 1 pound boneless, skinless turkey breast, cut into ¾" pieces
- 1 onion, finely chopped
- 1 sweet potato, peeled and cubed
- 1 teaspoon dried savory
- ¼ teaspoon salt
- 1 cup fresh or frozen and thawed peas
- ½ teaspoon freshly ground black pepper
- ¼ pound escarole, stems removed (about 2 cups packed)

*When only a hearty, home style soup will do, this one will fill the bill. Savory herbs and sweet potatoes make it deliciously different, and peas provide a bright splash of color.*

In a large saucepan, combine the broth, turkey, onion, sweet potato, savory, and salt. Bring to a boil over high heat. Reduce the heat to low, cover, and simmer for 20 minutes, stirring occasionally.

Add the peas and pepper. Simmer for 4 minutes. Stir in the escarole. Cook for 1 minute, or until the escarole is wilted.

**Makes 4 servings**

*Per serving: 206 calories, 32 g protein, 17 g carbohydrates, 2 g fat, 71 mg cholesterol, 5 g fiber, 784 mg sodium*

---

### COOKING TIP

To freeze a soup or stew: Let it cool, then pack in a freezer-quality plastic container. Be sure to leave ½" of head space to allow for expansion. To use, thaw overnight in the refrigerator. Transfer to a saucepan. Cover and cook, stirring frequently, over low heat for 15 minutes, or until hot.

# Curried Turkey and Rice Soup

3 cups chicken broth

2 cups water

2 carrots, thinly sliced

2 ribs celery, thinly sliced

⅓ cup brown rice

⅓ cup wild rice

¾ teaspoon curry powder

¼ teaspoon salt

2 tablespoons butter

1 pound skinless, boneless turkey breast, cut into ¾" pieces

2 cups thinly sliced mushrooms

1 cup buttermilk

*Curry powder gives this exuberant soup its exotic flavor. Wild rice and mushrooms become great partners for tender turkey, and buttermilk adds an unexpected richness.*

In a large saucepan, combine the broth, water, carrots, and celery. Bring to a boil over high heat. Stir in the brown rice, wild rice, curry powder, and salt. Reduce the heat to low, cover, and simmer for 25 minutes, stirring occasionally.

Meanwhile, melt the butter in a skillet over medium-high heat. Add the turkey and cook, stirring frequently, for 5 minutes, or until browned. Remove with a slotted spoon to a bowl. Add the mushrooms to the skillet and cook, stirring, for 5 minutes, or until lightly browned. Remove to the bowl with the turkey.

Stir the turkey and mushrooms into the broth mixture. Continue simmering for 15 minutes or until the rice is tender and the turkey is cooked.

Stir in the buttermilk. Cook for 1 minute, or until heated through.

**Makes 4 servings**

*Per serving: 320 calories, 29 g protein, 31 g carbohydrates, 11 g fat, 72 mg cholesterol, 4 g fiber, 774 mg sodium*

# Tomato Soup with Turkey

3 tablespoons olive oil

1 pound ground turkey breast

3 cloves garlic, minced

1 onion, finely chopped

1 rib celery, finely chopped

1 can (28 ounces) crushed tomatoes

1½ cups chicken broth

½ cup dry white wine

1 bay leaf

1 teaspoon dried marjoram

⅛ teaspoon ground red pepper

¼ cup chopped fresh basil

*Get ready for a really great tomato soup—one in which simple ingredients combine to create complex flavors. Assemble it in short order and savor the results.*

Heat the oil in a large saucepan over medium-high heat. Add the turkey, garlic, onion, and celery. Cook, stirring often, for 8 minutes, or until the turkey is browned and no longer pink, and the onion and celery are tender.

Stir in the tomatoes, broth, wine, bay leaf, marjoram, and pepper. Bring to a boil. Reduce the heat to low, cover, and simmer for 30 minutes.

Discard the bay leaf. Stir in the basil.

**Makes 4 servings**
*Per serving: 318 calories, 32 g protein, 18 g carbohydrates, 11 g fat, 71 mg cholesterol, 5 g fiber, 769 mg sodium*

# Traditional Beef-Barley Soup

⅓ cup unbleached all-purpose flour

1 pound beef stew meat

2 tablespoons olive oil

8 ounces mushrooms, thinly sliced (about 2 cups)

2 onions, finely chopped

1 rib celery, finely chopped

2 cups beef broth

2 cups water

3 tablespoons barley

1 carrot, finely chopped

1 bay leaf

2 teaspoons chopped fresh thyme or 1 teaspoon dried

½ teaspoon freshly ground black pepper

1 tablespoon soy sauce

*Ladle up some old-time goodness with this slow-simmer gem. All the ingredients are easy to find and preparation is a snap. Then kick back and enjoy a steaming bowlful.*

Place the flour in a resealable plastic bag. Add the beef, seal the bag, and toss to coat.

Heat the oil in a large saucepan over medium-high heat. Add the beef and cook, stirring frequently, for 8 minutes, or until browned. Add the mushrooms, onions, and celery. Cook, stirring occasionally, for 7 minutes, or until the mushrooms and onions are lightly browned.

Stir in the broth, water, barley, carrot, bay leaf, thyme, pepper, and soy sauce. Bring to a boil. Reduce the heat to low, cover, and simmer for 2 hours, or until the beef and barley are tender. Discard the bay leaf.

### Makes 4 servings

*Per serving: 391 calories, 39 g protein, 24 g carbohydrates, 16 g fat, 79 mg cholesterol, 4 g fiber, 757 mg sodium*

# Tex-Mex Meatball Soup

## Meatballs

1   pound lean ground beef
1   cup fresh bread crumbs
2   eggs, lightly beaten
2   cloves garlic, crushed
2   tablespoons chopped fresh cilantro
1   teaspoon chili powder
¼   teaspoon salt

## Soup

1   tablespoon olive oil
2   cloves garlic, minced
1   onion, chopped
1   large red bell pepper, chopped
8   ounces mushrooms, thinly sliced
1   can (14½ ounces) plum tomatoes, cut up
3   cups beef broth
1   cup fresh or frozen and thawed corn
1   cup canned black beans, rinsed and drained
¼   teaspoon crushed red pepper flakes
2   tablespoons chopped fresh cilantro
1   small avocado, cubed

*Impress hungry diners with this creative meatball dish. It highlights delightful border foods: tomatoes, corn, black beans, and bell peppers. To suit busy schedules, the chili-spiced meatballs can be cooked ahead and refrigerated.*

*To make the meatballs:* Preheat the oven to 425°F. Coat a broiler pan with cooking spray.

In a large bowl, combine the beef, bread crumbs, eggs, garlic, cilantro, chili powder, and salt. Shape into 1" balls. Place on the prepared broiler pan.

Bake the meatballs, turning occasionally, for 20 minutes, or until browned.

*To make the soup:* Heat the oil in a large saucepan over medium-high heat. Add the garlic, onion, pepper, and mushrooms. Cook, stirring occasionally, for 10 minutes, or until the vegetables are tender.

Stir in the tomatoes (with juice), broth, corn, beans, and pepper flakes. Bring to a boil. Add the meatballs. Reduce the heat to low, cover, and simmer for 15 minutes, or until meatballs are cooked throughout. Stir in the cilantro.

Top each serving with the avocado.

### Makes 6 servings

*Per serving: 488 calories, 26 g protein, 36 g carbohydrates, 27 g fat, 128 mg cholesterol, 7 g fiber, 880 mg sodium*

# Tortilla Soup

- 2 tablespoons olive oil
- 1 pound lean ground beef
- 4 cloves garlic, minced
- 1 onion, finely chopped
- 1 green bell pepper, finely chopped
- 3 cups chicken broth
- 1 can (28 ounces) crushed tomatoes
- 1 tablespoon dry sherry
- ¼ cup chopped fresh basil
- 2 teaspoons chili powder
- 1 teaspoon ground cumin
- 1 bay leaf
- ¼ cup chopped fresh cilantro
- 3 corn tortillas, cut into ½" strips
- 1 tablespoon lime juice
- ½ cup (2 ounces) shredded Monterey Jack cheese
- ½ cup (4 ounces) sour cream
- 1 small avocado, chopped

*Enjoy this trendy soup without venturing to Mexico City. Just like the versions served in fancy Mexican eateries, this recipe sings with zippy spices, tomatoes, Monterey Jack cheese, and, of course, toasted tortillas. Buen apetito!*

Heat the oil in a large saucepan over medium-high heat. Add the beef and cook, stirring often, for 8 minutes, or until no longer pink. Add the garlic, onion, and pepper. Cook, stirring occasionally, for 5 minutes, or until the vegetables are tender but not browned.

Add the broth, tomatoes, sherry, basil, chili powder, cumin, bay leaf, and 2 tablespoons of the cilantro. Bring just to a boil. Reduce the heat to low, cover, and simmer for 20 minutes. Discard the bay leaf.

Meanwhile, preheat the oven to 400°F. Arrange the tortilla strips on a baking sheet. Mist with olive oil cooking spray. Bake for 10 minutes, or until lightly browned.

Stir the lime juice and remaining 2 tablespoons of cilantro into the tomato mixture.

Serve the soup with the tortilla strips, cheese, sour cream, and avocado.

### Makes 6 servings
*Per serving: 455 calories, 21 g protein, 23 g carbohydrates, 33 g fat, 74 mg cholesterol, 6 g fiber, 772 mg sodium*

# Roasted Garlic Soup
# with Pork and Broccoli

4   bulbs garlic
3   tablespoons olive oil
4   cups chicken broth
1   pound pork tenderloin,
    cut into ¾" pieces
1   small onion, sliced
1   red bell pepper, chopped
4   ounces mushrooms,
    sliced (about 1 cup)
½   small bunch broccoli, cut
    into small florets (about
    1 cup)
2   teaspoons teriyaki sauce
½   teaspoon freshly ground
    black pepper

*Gently roasting garlic gives it a mild, almost sweet flavor. Paired with succulent pork tenderloin and fresh broccoli, this intriguing soup has a subtle, international flair.*

Preheat the oven to 350°F. Slice the top ¼" from each garlic bulb. Discard the tops. Lightly brush the bulbs with 1 tablespoon of the oil. Place in a shallow baking dish. Cover with foil.

Bake for 55 to 60 minutes. Remove the foil and bake for 10 minutes, or until the garlic skin is browned and the interior is very soft. Remove to a rack to cool.

When the garlic is cool enough to handle, squeeze the cloves into a food processor or blender. Discard the skin. Add 1 cup of the broth. Process until smooth.

Heat the remaining 2 tablespoons oil in a large saucepan over medium-high heat. Add the pork, onion, bell pepper, and mushrooms. Cook, stirring occasionally, for 15 minutes, or until the pork is lightly browned and the vegetables are tender.

Stir in the remainder of the broth, broccoli, garlic-broth mixture, teriyaki sauce, and pepper. Bring to a boil. Reduce the heat to low, cover, and simmer for 15 minutes, or until the pork is tender.

**Makes 6 servings**
*Per serving: 193 calories, 19 g protein, 9 g carbohydrates, 10 g fat, 50 mg cholesterol, 2 g fiber, 502 mg sodium*

# Asian Pork Noodle Soup

2   tablespoons peanut oil

1   pork tenderloin (about
    ¾ pound), cut into thin
    strips

4   scallions, thinly sliced

2   cloves garlic, minced

2   teaspoons grated fresh
    ginger

8   ounces mushrooms,
    thinly sliced

3   cups chicken broth

2   cups water

1   can (8 ounces) sliced
    water chestnuts, drained

2   tablespoons low-sodium
    soy sauce

¼   teaspoon Thai seasoning

4   ounces Chinese wheat
    noodles

8   ounces spinach, stems
    removed and coarsely
    chopped

1   carrot, shredded

*Capture the flavors of an Asian stir-fry in this splendid soup. Pork, mushrooms, water chestnuts, and Chinese noodles mingle in a delicate broth spiked with ginger and Thai seasoning.*

Heat the oil in a large saucepan over medium-high heat. Add the pork, scallions, garlic, ginger, and mushrooms. Cook, stirring occasionally, for 10 minutes, or until the pork and mushrooms are lightly browned.

Add the broth, water, water chestnuts, soy sauce, and Thai seasoning. Bring to a boil. Reduce the heat to low, cover, and simmer for 30 minutes, or until the pork is tender.

Stir in the noodles. Cook for 3 minutes or until almost tender. Stir in the spinach and carrot. Cook 2 minutes longer or until the spinach is wilted.

### Makes 4 servings

*Per serving: 292 calories, 25 g protein, 23 g carbohydrates, 13 g fat, 56 mg cholesterol, 9 g fiber, 996 mg sodium*

# Ham and Potato Chowder with Scallions

1     tablespoon olive oil

2     onions, chopped

2     tablespoons unbleached all-purpose flour

3     cups chicken broth

2     cups water

4     large potatoes, peeled and cubed

1     teaspoon dried marjoram

1     teaspoon mustard powder

¼     teaspoon curry powder

¼     teaspoon celery seeds

¼     teaspoon freshly ground black pepper

1⅔     cups milk

½     pound fully cooked lean ham, cut into ¾" pieces

6     scallions, sliced

*Creamy and comforting, this spud soup will warm your soul and please your palate. Serve with a crisp salad for a simple, satisfying supper in less than 30 minutes.*

Heat the oil in a large saucepan. Add the onions and cook, stirring occasionally, for 5 minutes, or until translucent. Stir in the flour and cook for 1 minute. Gradually stir in the broth until well-blended.

Add the water, potatoes, marjoram, mustard, curry, celery seeds, and pepper. Bring to a boil. Reduce the heat to low, cover, and simmer for 20 minutes, or until the potatoes are tender. Working in batches, transfer the vegetables to a blender or food processor and process until pureed. Return to the saucepan.

Stir in the milk, ham, and scallions. Gently simmer, stirring occasionally, for 5 minutes.

### Makes 6 servings
*Per serving: 201 calories, 14 g protein, 24 g carbohydrates, 7 g fat, 25 mg cholesterol, 3 g fiber, 900 mg sodium*

# ABUNDANT SEAFOOD SOUPS

# Shrimp and Mussel Chowder

1   **pound fresh mussels, washed and debearded**

1   **cup fish, vegetable, or chicken broth**

1   **cup bottled clam juice**

1   **bay leaf**

6   **sprigs thyme**

3   **cloves garlic, minced**

2   **tablespoons butter**

¼   **cup unbleached all-purpose flour**

2   **cups milk**

1   **red potato, cubed**

1   **rib celery, chopped**

1   **small green bell pepper, chopped**

1   **small red bell pepper, chopped**

1   **cup frozen corn, thawed**

1   **carrot, chopped**

¼   **pound medium shrimp, peeled and deveined**

¼   **pound cod, cut into 1" cubes**

**Hot-pepper sauce**

1   **tablespoon finely chopped fresh parsley**

*This colorful seafood lovers' dish combines three favorites—mussels, cod, and shrimp—all in a flavorful thyme-seasoned broth. If mussels aren't available, use clams and cook them as you would the mussels.*

In a large saucepan, combine the mussels, broth, clam juice, bay leaf, thyme, and garlic. Bring to a boil over medium-high heat. Reduce the heat to low, cover, and simmer for 10 minutes, or until the mussels open. Discard any unopened mussels.

Line a sieve or colander with cheesecloth. Strain the broth from the mussels and reserve. Discard the bay leaf, thyme sprigs, and garlic. Remove the mussels from the shells and reserve the mussels. Discard the shells.

Wash and dry the saucepan. Melt the butter in the saucepan over medium heat. Stir in the flour to make a smooth paste. Gradually whisk in the reserved mussel broth and the milk. Cook, whisking, over medium-low heat for 5 minutes, or until thickened.

Stir in the potato, celery, bell peppers, corn, and carrot. Cover and simmer for 20 minutes, or until the vegetables are tender.

Stir in the shrimp and cod. Simmer, covered, for 8 minutes, or until the fish is opaque. Season with the hot-pepper sauce. Stir in the parsley and mussels and serve immediately.

### Makes 4 servings
*Per serving: 388 calories, 33 g protein, 39 g carbohydrates, 13 g fat, 113 mg cholesterol, 4 g fiber, 807 mg sodium*

# Creole Catfish Chowder

2 tablespoons butter

6 scallions, chopped

2 ribs celery, chopped

2 large cloves garlic, minced

1 red bell pepper, chopped

2 cups fish, vegetable, or chicken broth

1 can (14 ounces) diced tomatoes

½ pound green beans, cut into 2" pieces

1 teaspoon dried marjoram leaves

1 teaspoon dried oregano leaves

½ teaspoon Creole seasoning

1 pound catfish, cut into 1" pieces

1 tablespoon chopped fresh parsley

*This irresistible dish sings with signature Creole flavors—scallions, celery, bell pepper, parsley, and, of course, peppery Creole seasoning. For the most authentic flavor, stick with catfish. If catfish isn't available, use another mild white fish such as cod or haddock.*

Melt the butter in a large saucepan over medium-high heat. Add the scallions, celery, garlic, and pepper. Cook, stirring occasionally, for 8 minutes, or until the vegetables are lightly browned.

Stir in the broth, tomatoes (with juice), green beans, marjoram, oregano, and Creole seasoning. Bring to a boil. Reduce the heat to low, cover, and simmer for 15 minutes, or until the vegetables are tender.

Add the fish. Cover and simmer for 10 minutes, or until the fish is opaque. Stir in the parsley.

**Makes 4 servings**

*Per serving: 249 calories, 24 g protein, 19 g carbohydrates, 10 g fat, 121 mg cholesterol, 5 g fiber, 629 mg sodium*

# Scallop and Clam Chowder

2   tablespoons olive oil

4   shallots, sliced

3   cloves garlic, minced

4   cups fish, vegetable, or chicken broth

4   plum tomatoes, chopped

1   bay leaf

½   teaspoon dried rosemary, crushed

¼   teaspoon yellow mustard seeds

¼   teaspoon salt

½   pound sea scallops

1   dozen littleneck clams, scrubbed

½   pound haddock fillets, cut into 1" pieces

¼   cup chopped fresh parsley

¼   cup (2 ounces) grated Asiago cheese (optional)

*This lively version of cioppino (chuh-PEE-noh), a seafood-laden dish created by San Francisco's Italian immigrants, features scallops, little-neck clams, and haddock. Serve it with sourdough bread to sop up the wonderful rosemary-tomato broth.*

Heat the oil in a large saucepan over medium-high heat. Add the shallots and garlic. Cook, stirring occasionally, for 6 minutes, or until lightly browned.

Stir in the broth, tomatoes, bay leaf, rosemary, mustard seeds, and salt. Bring to a boil. Reduce the heat to low, cover, and simmer for 30 minutes.

Add the scallops, clams, and haddock. Simmer gently for 5 minutes, or until the scallops are opaque, the clams open, and the fish is opaque.

Discard the bay leaf and any unopened clams. Stir in the parsley. Serve with the cheese, if using.

**Makes 4 servings**

*Per serving: 272 calories, 33 g protein, 13 g carbohydrates, 11 g fat, 80 mg cholesterol, 2 g fiber, 1,060 mg sodium*

# Manhattan Clam Chowder

2    slices bacon

2    ribs celery, thinly sliced

1    onion, finely chopped

1    clove garlic, minced

2    cans (6½ ounces each) chopped clams

¾    cup bottled clam juice

1    large potato, peeled and cubed

2    carrots, chopped

1    teaspoon dried thyme

1    bay leaf

1    can (14 ounces) diced tomatoes

2–3    drops hot-pepper sauce

*Bacon and hot-pepper sauce pump up the usual tomato-clam flavors in this delightful rendition of the famous New York–style chowder. The recipe calls for easy-to-use canned clams, but you could substitute two dozen littleneck clams if you prefer.*

Cook the bacon in a large saucepan over medium heat until crisp. Transfer to a plate lined with paper towels. Crumble into a small bowl. Set aside.

Add the celery, onion, and garlic to the bacon drippings in the saucepan. Cook, stirring occasionally, for 5 minutes, or until the onion and celery are tender.

Drain the juice from the clams into a small bowl. Set the clams aside and add the juice to the onion mixture. Stir in the bottled clam juice, potato, carrots, thyme, and bay leaf. Bring to a boil. Reduce the heat to low, cover, and simmer for 20 minutes, or until the vegetables are tender.

Stir in the tomatoes (with juice). Bring to a boil over high heat. Reduce the heat to low, add the reserved clams, cover, and simmer for 8 minutes. Discard the bay leaf. Season with the hot-pepper sauce. Stir in the bacon.

## Makes 4 servings

*Per serving: 138 calories, 10 g protein, 22 g carbohydrates, 2 g fat, 20 mg cholesterol, 4 g fiber, 1,001 mg sodium*

# New England Clam Chowder

1⅓ cups water

2 dozen littleneck clams, scrubbed

2 tablespoons butter

4 potatoes, peeled and chopped

2 large onions, chopped

2 ounces lean ham, finely chopped

1 clove garlic, minced

1½ cups bottled clam juice

1 teaspoon dried thyme leaves

1⅓ cups milk

1 scallion, thinly sliced

*Here's the best-ever creamy chowder. It's brimming with clams and potatoes and seasoned to please with ham and thyme. Pureed potatoes ensure a thick broth.*

Bring the water to a boil in a large saucepan over high heat. Add the clams. Reduce the heat to medium low, cover, and simmer for 5 minutes, or until the clams open. Use a slotted spoon to remove the clams to a bowl. Discard any unopened clams. Strain the liquid through a cheesecloth-lined strainer into a large bowl. Set aside the liquid. Remove the clams from the shells and discard the shells.

Melt the butter in the same saucepan over medium heat. Add the potatoes, onions, ham, and garlic. Cook, stirring occasionally, for 5 minutes.

Stir in the reserved clam broth, clam juice, and thyme. Bring to a boil over medium-high heat. Reduce the heat to low, cover, and simmer for 20 minutes, or until the potatoes are tender. Let cool slightly.

Transfer half the mixture to a food processor or blender. Process until pureed. Return to the pan. Stir in the milk. Over medium heat bring to a simmer. Stir in the reserved clams. Sprinkle with the scallion.

**Makes 4 servings**

*Per serving: 275 calories, 15 g protein, 36 g carbohydrates, 9 g fat, 42 mg cholesterol, 4 g fiber, 487 mg sodium*

# Salmon Chowder with Olives

¾ pound salmon fillets, skinned

4 cups fish, vegetable, or chicken broth

2 cloves garlic, minced

3 potatoes, peeled and cut into ½" pieces

1 leek, thinly sliced

1 cup frozen peas, thawed

3 ounces cream cheese, softened

½ cup milk

¼ cup unbleached all-purpose flour

10 kalamata olives, pitted and thinly sliced

1 tablespoon chopped fresh dill

⅛ teaspoon cracked black pepper

*Never had salmon chowder? Here's a version that will make regular appearances on your table. A generous chunk of cream cheese gives this chowder a creamy, rich taste. Dill and olives give it pizzazz.*

Remove and discard the bones from the salmon. Cut it into 1" pieces.

In a large saucepan, bring the broth and garlic to a boil over medium-high heat. Add the potatoes and leek. Reduce the heat to low, cover, and simmer for 15 minutes, or until the potatoes are almost tender.

Add the salmon and simmer, covered, for 5 minutes, or until the fish is opaque. Stir in the peas.

In a small bowl, stir together the cream cheese, milk, and flour. Stir in ½ cup of the hot salmon mixture into the bowl. Gradually stir the cream cheese mixture into the salmon mixture in the saucepan.

Bring to a boil over medium-high heat, stirring constantly. Reduce the heat to low and cook, stirring, for 2 minutes. Stir in the olives, dill, and pepper.

**Makes 4 servings**

*Per serving: 356 calories, 27 g protein, 38 g carbohydrates, 12 g fat, 62 mg cholesterol, 5 g fiber, 796 mg sodium*

# Lobster Bisque

2 tablespoons butter

1 onion, finely chopped

2 tablespoons unbleached all-purpose flour

3½ cups fish, vegetable, or chicken broth

½ cup tomato puree

¼ cup sherry

¼ teaspoon salt

1 pound lobster tails, shells removed and cut into 1" pieces

1¼ cups milk

¼ teaspoon hot-pepper sauce

1 teaspoon paprika

2 plum tomatoes, chopped

1 tablespoon chopped fresh parsley

*Silky and full-flavored, bisques make any meal an elegant occasion. This easy version uses sherry in lieu of the more traditional white wine. Lobster tails—instead of live whole lobsters—make preparation a snap.*

Melt the butter in a large saucepan over medium-high heat. Add the onion and cook, stirring occasionally, for 5 minutes, or until tender. Stir in the flour and cook, stirring constantly, for 3 minutes, or until lightly browned.

Stir in the broth, tomato puree, sherry, and salt. Bring to a boil. Reduce the heat to low, cover, and simmer for 10 minutes. Add the lobster and simmer, covered, for 6 minutes, or until the lobster is opaque.

Stir in the milk, hot-pepper sauce, and paprika. Cook over medium heat for 3 minutes, or until heated through. Stir in the plum tomatoes and parsley.

## Makes 4 servings

*Per serving: 269 calories, 26 g protein, 17 g carbohydrates, 11 g fat, 135 mg cholesterol, 3 g fiber, 913 mg sodium*

# Creamy Shrimp Bisque

2   tablespoons butter

1   onion, finely chopped

1   rib celery, finely chopped

2   tablespoons unbleached
    all-purpose flour

3   cups fish, vegetable, or
    chicken broth

1   cup tomato puree

¼   cup dry white wine

¼   teaspoon salt

1   pound medium shrimp,
    peeled and deveined

1½  cups milk

½   teaspoon freshly grated
    nutmeg

2   scallions, sliced

*Here's a unique bisque that gets its richness from tomato puree. Serve as a light lunch with whole wheat bread and a salad, or serve as a first course for a more formal meal.*

Melt the butter in a large saucepan over medium-high heat. Add the onion and celery. Cook, stirring occasionally, for 5 minutes, or until tender. Stir in the flour and cook for 3 minutes, or until light brown.

Stir in the broth, tomato puree, wine, and salt. Simmer, covered, for 8 minutes. Pour the mixture, in batches if necessary, into a food processor or blender. Process until smooth. Return to the saucepan. Over medium heat, bring to a simmer. Add the shrimp, cover, and simmer for 4 minutes, or until the shrimp is opaque.

Stir in the milk and nutmeg. Cook for 3 minutes, or until heated through.

Top each serving with the scallions.

### Makes 4 servings

*Per serving: 283 calories, 29 g protein, 17 g carbohydrates, 11 g fat, 196 mg cholesterol, 3 g fiber, 952 mg sodium*

# Asian-Style Shrimp Soup

1 tablespoon vegetable oil

2 ounces mushrooms, thinly sliced

2 cloves garlic, minced

1 small onion, finely chopped

1 tablespoon finely chopped fresh ginger

3 cups fish, vegetable, or chicken broth

3 cups water

1 tablespoon teriyaki sauce

1 tablespoon sherry

¼ teaspoon Szechuan seasoning

¾ pound medium shrimp, peeled and deveined

¼ head Napa cabbage, thinly sliced

1 carrot, shredded

1 rib celery, thinly sliced

1 small red bell pepper, thinly sliced

¾ cup baby spinach leaves

*Take-out food fades fast next to this singular soup, which is light and fresh tasting and chock-full of colorful vegetables. Teriyaki flavors dominate.*

Heat the oil in a large saucepan over medium-high heat. Add the mushrooms, garlic, onion, and ginger. Cook, stirring frequently, for 4 minutes, or until tender.

Add the broth, water, teriyaki sauce, sherry, and Szechuan seasoning. Bring to a boil. Add the shrimp. Reduce the heat to low, cover, and simmer for 4 minutes.

Stir in the cabbage, carrot, celery, pepper, and spinach. Cover and simmer for 4 minutes, or until the shrimp are opaque and the vegetables are tender.

**Makes 4 servings**

*Per serving: 170 calories, 21 g protein, 10 g carbohydrates, 6 g fat, 130 mg cholesterol, 4 g fiber, 756 mg sodium*

---
**COOKING TIP**

Don't cry over onions. Instead, cut them with a very sharp knife to avoid crushing the flesh and releasing the pungent juices. As you work, dip the knife in ice water to wash away the juices.

---

# BEST-EVER
# **BEAN**
# SOUPS

# White Bean and Carrot Soup

2    **large russet potatoes, peeled and chopped**

6    **cups vegetable or chicken broth**

2    **tablespoons olive oil**

1    **onion, chopped**

3    **cloves garlic, minced**

1    **can (14½–19 ounces) small white beans, rinsed and drained**

2    **carrots, chopped**

½    **cup milk**

2    **tablespoons chopped fresh parsley**

¼    **teaspoon salt**

¼    **teaspoon ground white pepper**

*Can a bean soup be elegant, aristocratic? Absolutely. In this pleasant soup, small white beans float in a light broth to achieve the sophisticated touch. Serve with seasoned croutons or crisp crackers.*

Place the potatoes and 2 cups of the broth in a medium saucepan. Bring to a boil over high heat. Reduce the heat to low, cover, and simmer for 15 minutes, or until tender. Remove from the heat. Using a fork, potato masher, or handheld immersion blender, mash until free of lumps. Set aside.

Heat the oil in a large saucepan over medium heat. Add the onion and cook, stirring occasionally, for 10 minutes, or until golden. Add the garlic and cook for 1 minute.

Add the beans, carrots, and the remaining 4 cups broth. Bring to a boil over medium-high heat. Reduce the heat to low, cover, and simmer for 20 minutes, or until the carrots are tender.

Stir in the potatoes, milk, parsley, salt, and pepper. Cook, stirring occasionally, for 5 minutes, or until heated through.

**Makes 6 servings**
*Per serving: 223 calories, 11 g protein, 35 g carbohydrates, 6 g fat, 2 mg cholesterol, 8 g fiber, 694 mg sodium*

# Black Bean Soup

1    **pound black beans, soaked overnight**

3    **cups vegetable or chicken broth**

7    **cups water**

4    **cloves garlic, minced**

2    **teaspoons dried oregano**

1    **teaspoon cumin seeds**

1    **teaspoon coriander seeds**

¼    **teaspoon ground red pepper**

2    **tablespoons olive oil**

1    **large onion, chopped**

    **Juice of ½ lime**

2    **tablespoons Worcestershire sauce**

½    **teaspoon salt**

2    **tablespoons chopped roasted red peppers**

¼    **cup chopped fresh cilantro**

*Cumin, cilantro, and roasted peppers give this hearty southwestern classic its stunning flavor. For a contrast of textures, serve with white corn tortilla chips.*

Drain the beans. In a large saucepan, over high heat, bring the beans, broth, and water to a boil. Reduce the heat to low, cover, and simmer for 2 to 2½ hours, or until the beans are tender.

With a mortar and pestle, grind the garlic, oregano, cumin seeds, coriander seeds, and ground red pepper into a paste. If you don't have a mortar and pestle, place these ingredients in a resealable plastic bag, seal the bag, and mash with a rolling pin.

Heat the oil in a skillet over medium heat. Add the onion and spice paste. Cook for 5 minutes or until tender, stirring occasionally. Stir in the lime juice, Worcestershire sauce, and salt.

Stir the onion mixture into the beans. Simmer, uncovered, for 30 minutes.

Allow to cool slightly. Transfer half of the bean mixture to a food processor or blender. Process until pureed. Return to the pan. Stir in the roasted red peppers and cilantro.

### Makes 6 servings

*Per serving: 318 calories, 18 g protein, 52 g carbohydrates, 6 g fat, 1 mg cholesterol, 13 g fiber, 548 mg sodium*

# Pasta e Fagioli

2    tablespoons olive oil

1    large onion, chopped

4    cloves garlic, minced

2    cups vegetable or chicken broth

2    cups water

½    cup ditalini or elbow macaroni

1    can (14½ ounces) stewed tomatoes

1    can (14½–19 ounces) cannelini beans, rinsed and drained

1    cup spinach leaves

1    tablespoon chopped fresh basil

¼    cup (2 ounces) grated Romano or Parmesan cheese

*This Italian country-style soup is a hearty meal served with a Caesar salad and garlic bread. Stock your pantry with the main ingredients for last-minute dinner solutions.*

Heat the oil in a large saucepan over medium-high heat. Add the onion and cook, stirring occasionally, for 5 minutes, or until soft. Add the garlic and cook for 1 minute.

Add the broth and water and bring to a boil. Stir in the macaroni and return to a boil. Reduce the heat to low and simmer for 8 minutes, or just until the macaroni is tender.

Stir in the tomatoes (with juice) and beans and return to a simmer. Add the spinach and basil and cook for 2 minutes or until the spinach is wilted.

Serve with the cheese.

**Makes 4 servings**

*Per serving: 387 calories, 16 g protein, 52 g carbohydrates, 13 g fat, 5 mg cholesterol, 9 g fiber, 841 mg sodium*

# Curried Chickpea Soup

3    **large cloves garlic, minced**

2    **onions, finely chopped**

4    **cups vegetable or chicken broth**

2    **cans (14½–19 ounces) chickpeas, rinsed and drained**

2    **carrots, chopped**

2    **teaspoons curry powder**

½    **teaspoon turmeric**

½    **teaspoon salt**

¼    **teaspoon ground ginger**

¼    **teaspoon freshly ground black pepper**

½    **cup milk**

1    **tablespoon chopped fresh parsley**

8    **slices French bread**

*Chickpeas (also known as garbanzo beans) have a special down-to-earth flavor that blends perfectly with a spicy curry. The word curry comes from the Indian kari, meaning "sauce," and curry powder, a blend of up to 20 spices, is an integral part of every curry recipe. Serve this one with a salad of crisp greens.*

In a large saucepan over medium heat, cook the garlic, onion, and 3 tablespoons of the broth for 5 minutes, or until the onion is translucent.

Stir in the chickpeas, carrots, curry powder, turmeric, salt, ginger, pepper, and remaining broth. Bring to a boil over high heat. Reduce the heat to low, cover, and simmer for 15 minutes. Let cool slightly.

Transfer to a blender or food processor, working in batches if necessary. Process until smooth. Return to the pan. Stir in the milk and parsley.

Toast the bread and serve atop each serving.

### Makes 6 servings

*Per serving: 370 calories, 17 g protein, 66 g carbohydrates, 5 g fat, 2 mg cholesterol, 11 g fiber, 903 mg sodium*

# Pinto Bean and Fresh Vegetable Soup

| | |
|---|---|
| 2 | tablespoons olive oil |
| 3 | cloves garlic, minced |
| 2 | carrots, thinly sliced |
| 1 | onion, chopped |
| 1 | tablespoon chopped fresh rosemary or 1 teaspoon dried |
| ¼ | teaspoon salt |
| ¼ | teaspoon freshly ground black pepper |
| 4 | cups vegetable or chicken broth |
| 1 | potato, peeled and cubed |
| 1 | can (14½–19 ounces) pinto beans, rinsed and drained |
| 1 | small zucchini, chopped |

*Create a fresh stir with this chunky soup. Aromatic rosemary is assertive, but plays very well with mild-mannered potatoes, zucchini, and pinto beans.*

Heat the oil in a large saucepan over medium-high heat. Add the garlic, carrots, onion, rosemary, salt, and pepper. Cook, stirring occasionally, for 2 minutes, or until the vegetables are soft.

Stir in the broth, potato, and beans. Bring to a boil. Reduce the heat to low, cover, and simmer for 8 minutes. Stir in the zucchini. Cook, covered, for 3 minutes, or until the vegetables are tender. Using a potato masher, mash to a chunky texture.

**Makes 4 servings**
*Per serving: 232 calories, 14 g protein, 34 g carbohydrates, 8 g fat, 0 mg cholesterol, 9 g fiber, 828 mg sodium*

## COOKING TIP

An easy way to peel garlic is to crush it with the broad side of a heavy knife. The peel will slip right off.

# Split Pea Soup

1 cup dried green split peas, sorted and rinsed

4 cups vegetable or chicken broth

1 small onion, chopped

1 rib celery, chopped

1 carrot, thinly sliced

3 ounces chopped, cooked lean ham (about ½ cup)

6 sprigs thyme

1 bay leaf

¼ teaspoon freshly ground black pepper

1 tablespoon minced fresh dill

*Many traditional split pea recipes call for a ham bone simmered for hours. This updated version uses lean cooked ham for quicker preparation. Fresh dill adds pizzazz.*

Place the split peas and broth in a large saucepan. Bring to a boil over high heat. Reduce the heat to low, cover, and simmer for 45 minutes, stirring occasionally.

Add the onion, celery, carrot, ham, thyme, bay leaf, and pepper. Simmer, covered, for 45 minutes, stirring occasionally. Stir in the dill.

Discard the thyme sprigs and bay leaf.

### Makes 4 servings
*Per serving: 225 calories, 16 g protein, 32 g carbohydrates, 5 g fat, 11 mg cholesterol, 14 g fiber, 883 mg sodium*

### COOKING TIP

Fresh and dried herbs may be used interchangeably (with the exception of cilantro, which loses its flavor when dried). Always use three times as much fresh as dried (and one-third as much dried as fresh) when substituting in recipes. Drying concentrates the flavor so less is needed.

# Minestrone

2　tablespoons olive oil
1　onion, chopped
3　cloves garlic, minced
5　cups vegetable or chicken broth
1　small zucchini, chopped
1　cup cut green beans
1　cup frozen corn, thawed
1　teaspoon grated lemon peel
½　teaspoon dried rosemary
1　teaspoon dried Italian seasoning
½　teaspoon salt
¼　teaspoon freshly ground black pepper
1　can (14½ ounces) stewed tomatoes
1　can (15–19 ounces) cannellini beans, rinsed and drained
1　can (15–19 ounces) red kidney beans, rinsed and drained
2　tablespoons chopped fresh basil or 2 teaspoons dried

*Every region of Italy has its own version of minestrone, which in Italian means "big soup." This rendition is chock-full of vegetables and beans—three kinds of beans, to be exact. Serve with your favorite semolina bread for a complete meal.*

Heat the oil in a large saucepan over medium-high heat. Add the onion and cook, stirring occasionally, for 5 minutes, or until soft. Add the garlic and cook for 1 minute.

Stir in the broth, zucchini, green beans, corn, lemon peel, rosemary, Italian seasoning, salt, and pepper. Bring to a boil. Reduce the heat to low, cover, and simmer for 10 minutes, or until the vegetables are tender.

Stir in the tomatoes (with juice) and beans. Simmer, covered, for 30 minutes. Stir in the basil.

## Makes 6 servings
*Per serving: 295 calories, 16 g protein, 49 g carbohydrates, 6 g fat, 1 mg cholesterol, 15 g fiber, 878 mg sodium*

# Balsamic-Lentil Soup

2 tablespoons olive oil

1 onion, chopped

2 cloves garlic, minced

3 cups beef, vegetable, or chicken broth

3 cups water

1 can (14½ ounces) diced tomatoes

1 cup dried lentils, sorted and rinsed

1 bay leaf

2 cups chopped escarole

2 tablespoons balsamic vinegar

1 teaspoon mild-pepper sauce

*Try this delicious revision of a classic soup. Here, escarole, a somewhat bitter green, mingles with earthy lentils in a broth that's kissed with balsamic vinegar. The results? A humble soup with captivating dimension.*

Heat the oil in a large saucepan over medium-high heat. Add the onion and cook, stirring occasionally, for 5 minutes, or until soft. Add the garlic and cook for 1 minute.

Add the broth, water, tomatoes (with juice), lentils, and bay leaf. Bring to a boil. Reduce the heat to low, cover, and simmer for 40 minutes, or until the lentils are tender.

Remove and discard the bay leaf. Stir in the escarole, vinegar, and mild-pepper sauce. Cook for 5 minutes to blend the flavors.

**Makes 4 servings**

*Per serving: 285 calories, 17 g protein, 39 g carbohydrates, 9 g fat, 0 mg cholesterol, 17 g fiber, 860 mg sodium*

**COOKING TIP**

Balsamic vinegar gets its mellow, sweet flavor from being aged in wooden barrels for years. This dark brown Italian vinegar is delicious stirred into soups and stews and, of course, drizzled on salads.

# Three-Bean Soup

5 cups vegetable or chicken broth

1 can (14½ ounces) Italian stewed tomatoes

1 can (14½–19 ounces) red kidney beans, rinsed and drained

1 can (14½–19 ounces) pinto beans, rinsed and drained

2 onions, chopped

3 cloves garlic, minced

2 teaspoons dried rosemary

1 teaspoon dried oregano

1 teaspoon dried savory

½ teaspoon freshly ground black pepper

¼ teaspoon salt

2 cups cut green beans

1 turnip, peeled and cut into ½" pieces

*The flavor secret to this sturdy soup? A trio of herbs—oregano, rosemary, and savory. Best of all, it's an easy everyday dish that's worthy of company.*

Place the broth, tomatoes (with juice), kidney beans, pinto beans, onions, garlic, rosemary, oregano, savory, pepper, and salt in a large saucepan. Bring to a boil over high heat. Reduce the heat to low, cover, and simmer for 20 minutes, stirring occasionally.

Add the green beans and turnip. Simmer, covered, for 15 minutes, or until the turnip is tender.

### Makes 6 servings

*Per serving: 175 calories, 10 g protein, 34 g carbohydrates, 2 g fat, 1 mg cholesterol, 11 g fiber, 947 mg sodium*

---

### COOKING TIP

A quick way to "cut" fresh green beans into pieces is to "snap" or break them. If you prefer cutting, line up six at a time on a cutting board and cut all six at once.

# COUNTRY-STYLE
# VEGETABLE
# SOUPS

# Corn Chowder

1 tablespoon olive oil

1 onion, finely chopped

2 cloves garlic, minced

1 cup vegetable or chicken broth

1 can (15 ounces) cream-style corn

1 cup fresh or frozen and thawed corn

1 can (14 ounces) diced tomatoes

1 tablespoon fresh thyme leaves or 1 teaspoon dried

½ cup milk

¼ cup chopped roasted red peppers

¼ teaspoon freshly ground black pepper

1 teaspoon hot-pepper sauce

*Use farm-fresh corn in season to enhance this country-classic recipe. Making it is a breeze. Eating it is a joy.*

Heat the oil in a large saucepan over medium-high heat. Add the onion and cook, stirring occasionally, for 5 minutes, or until soft. Add the garlic and cook for 1 minute.

Add the broth, cream-style corn, fresh or frozen corn, tomatoes (with juice), and thyme. Bring to a boil. Reduce the heat to low, cover, and simmer for 10 minutes. Stir in the milk, red peppers, black pepper, and hot-pepper sauce. Cook for 3 minutes, or until heated through.

## Makes 4 servings

*Per serving: 193 calories, 7 g protein, 37 g carbohydrates, 6 g fat, 5 mg cholesterol, 4 g fiber, 889 mg sodium*

---

### COOKING TIP

When fresh corn is in season and readily available, use it instead of frozen corn. For one cupful, simply slice the kernels off two or three cobs.

# French-Style Vegetable Soup

4   cups vegetable or chicken broth

2   cups water

1   can (14½–19 ounces) small white beans, rinsed and drained

1   large tomato, seeded and chopped

2   leeks, thinly sliced

1   small zucchini, thinly sliced

4   ounces mushrooms, sliced

8   ounces green beans, cut into 1" pieces

1   small butternut squash, cubed

2   tablespoons chopped fresh parsley or 1 tablespoon dried

2   teaspoons chopped fresh basil or 1 teaspoon dried

2   cloves garlic, minced

½   teaspoon freshly ground black pepper

1   cup thin noodles

*Country-fresh takes on new meaning when you taste this simple and delicious soup. Angel-hair pasta makes an excellent substitute for the thin noodles, if you wish. Serve with a good, crusty bread.*

In a large saucepan, combine the broth, water, beans, tomato, leeks, zucchini, mushrooms, green beans, squash, parsley, basil, garlic, and pepper. Bring to a boil over medium-high heat.

Reduce the heat to low, cover, and simmer for 12 minutes, or until the vegetables are tender. Stir in the noodles. Cook, uncovered, for 5 minutes, or until the noodles are tender.

**Makes 4 servings**

*Per serving: 296 calories, 22 g protein, 60 g carbohydrates, 2 g fat, 10 mg cholesterol, 13 g fiber, 701 mg sodium*

---

**COOKING TIP**

To seed tomatoes: Cut them in half horizontally. Gently squeeze the halves over a sieve and bowl. Discard the seeds and reserve the juice for your favorite recipe.

# Mediterranean Eggplant Soup

1   **medium eggplant, peeled and chopped**

2   **tablespoons olive oil**

1   **small yellow squash, halved lengthwise and thinly sliced**

1   **onion, thinly sliced and separated into rings**

1   **green bell pepper, chopped**

2   **cloves garlic, minced**

4   **cups vegetable or chicken broth**

2   **tomatoes, seeded and diced**

2   **slices dry French bread, cubed**

1   **teaspoon dried herbs de Provence (see note on page 101)**

½   **teaspoon freshly ground black pepper**

2   **tablespoons minced fresh parsley**

¼   **cup crumbled feta cheese**

*Ratatouille, a traditional staple of Provence, was the inspiration for this deliciously thick, peasant-style soup. For a change of pace, try crumbled blue cheese or Roquefort instead of the feta cheese.*

Place the eggplant in a 3-quart baking dish. Cover with vented plastic wrap and microwave on high for 5 minutes, or until tender.

Meanwhile, heat the oil in a large saucepan over medium-high heat. Add the squash, onion, and bell pepper. Cook for 5 minutes, or until the vegetables are lightly browned.

Add the eggplant and garlic and cook for 3 minutes, stirring occasionally.

Add the broth, tomatoes, bread, herbs de Provence, and black pepper. Bring to a boil. Reduce the heat to low. Cover and simmer for 15 minutes, or until the vegetables are tender. Stir in the parsley.

Serve with cheese.

**Makes 4 servings**
*Per serving: 198 calories, 11 g protein, 26 g carbohydrates, 10 g fat, 9 mg cholesterol, 7 g fiber, 864 mg sodium*

# French Onion Soup

2    tablespoons olive oil

8    large sweet onions, thinly sliced and separated into rings

2    tablespoons unbleached all-purpose flour

¼    teaspoon freshly ground black pepper

4    cups beef or vegetable broth

2    cups water

    Mild-pepper sauce

4    slices French bread, lightly toasted

½    cup (4 ounces) shredded smoked Gouda cheese

¼    cup minced fresh parsley

*Traditionally, this onion-packed soup is topped with bread and Swiss cheese. For an exciting change of pace, this version features smoky Gouda on top of the bread.*

Heat the oil in a large saucepan over medium-high heat. Add the onions and cook, stirring frequently, for 5 minutes. Reduce the heat to medium low, cover, and cook for 10 minutes, or until very soft.

Uncover the pan and raise the heat to medium. Cook, stirring frequently, for 30 minutes, or until the onions are golden and almost caramel colored.

Sprinkle the flour and pepper over the onions and stir to combine. Pour in the broth and water, stirring well to smooth out the lumps. Bring to a boil.

Reduce the heat to low, cover, and simmer for 30 minutes, stirring occasionally. Stir in the mild-pepper sauce.

Preheat the oven to 425°F.

Ladle the soup into 4 oven-safe soup bowls. Top each serving with the bread, cheese, and parsley. Bake for 5 minutes, or until the cheese is melted and bubbly.

**Makes 4 servings**

*Per serving: 328 calories, 18 g protein, 37 g carbohydrates, 16 g fat, 32 mg cholesterol, 5 g fiber, 1,060 mg sodium*

# Ginger Carrot Soup

4 cups vegetable or chicken broth

½ cup orange juice

1 pound carrots, chopped

1 russet potato, peeled and chopped

1 small onion, chopped

1 tablespoon grated fresh ginger

1 teaspoon grated orange peel

1 cup buttermilk

2 tablespoons honey

¼ teaspoon salt

¼ teaspoon ground nutmeg

Pinch of ground red pepper

*Spiced with ginger, nutmeg, and just a pinch of ground red pepper, this creamy soup has a subtle warmth—one that'll chase the chills while pleasing the palate. Serve with a green salad and biscuits for a complete, but light, meal.*

In a large saucepan, combine the broth, orange juice, carrots, potato, onion, ginger, and orange peel. Bring to a boil over high heat. Reduce the heat to low, cover, and simmer for 20 minutes, or until the carrots and potato are tender. Let cool for 5 minutes.

Working in batches, puree the carrot mixture in a food processor or blender. Return to a saucepan.

Stir in the buttermilk, honey, salt, nutmeg, and pepper. Cook for 3 minutes, or until heated through.

**Makes 6 servings**

*Per serving: 103 calories, 7 g protein, 23 g carbohydrates, 1 g fat, 2 mg cholesterol, 4 g fiber, 616 mg sodium*

# Creamy Potato and Squash Soup

2　tablespoons olive oil

1　onion, chopped

3　cups chicken broth

1　tart apple, peeled and chopped

1　russet potato, peeled and chopped

2　cloves garlic, minced

1　package (12 ounces) frozen pureed winter squash, thawed

½　cup milk

¼　teaspoon ground cinnamon

¼　teaspoon salt

　　Pinch of ground red pepper

*Potatoes and winter squash play a delectable duet in this pureed soup. If you have extra, it reheats quite nicely for another enjoyable meal.*

Heat the oil in a large saucepan over medium heat. Add the onion. Cook, stirring occasionally, for 5 minutes, or until soft.

Add the broth, apple, potato, and garlic. Bring to a boil. Reduce the heat to low, cover, and simmer for 15 minutes, or until the potato is tender. Stir in the squash.

Working in batches, puree the mixture in a blender or food processor. Return to the pan. Stir in the milk, cinnamon, salt, and pepper. Cook 3 minutes, or until heated through.

**Makes 6 servings**

*Per serving: 119 calories, 3 g protein, 17 g carbohydrates, 6 g fat, 3 mg cholesterol, 4 g fiber, 395 mg sodium*

# Curried Broccoli and Cauliflower Soup

2 tablespoons olive oil

1 large onion, chopped

1 large rib celery, chopped

4 cups vegetable or chicken broth

3 potatoes, chopped

1 tablespoon spicy brown mustard

1 teaspoon curry powder

¼ teaspoon freshly ground black pepper

½ bunch broccoli, cut into small florets (about 1½ cups)

½ head cauliflower, cut into small florets (about 1½ cups)

1 cup milk

½ cup (4 ounces) shredded extra-sharp Cheddar cheese

*No need to travel to India for a good curried soup. This one features two favorite vegetables—tender broccoli and snow-white cauliflower. Cheddar cheese lends a mellow smoothness.*

Heat the oil in a large saucepan over medium-high heat. Add the onion and celery. Cook, stirring occasionally, for 5 minutes, or until soft.

Add the broth, potatoes, mustard, curry powder, and pepper. Bring to a boil. Reduce the heat to low, cover, and simmer for 15 minutes, or until the potatoes are tender.

Transfer 2 cups of the mixture to a blender. Process until smooth. Return to the pan, and add the broccoli and cauliflower. Cook, stirring frequently, for 5 minutes.

Add the milk and cheese. Cook, stirring frequently, for 3 minutes, or until the cheese melts.

**Makes 4 servings**

*Per serving: 273 calories, 15 g protein, 29 g carbohydrates, 14 g fat, 23 mg cholesterol, 6 g fiber, 877 mg sodium*

**Cream of Tomato Soup on page 70**

# Creamy Spinach Soup

4  cups water

1  package (10 ounces) frozen peas, thawed

2  cups vegetable or chicken broth

1  package (10 ounces) frozen chopped spinach, thawed

¼  teaspoon freshly ground nutmeg

¼  teaspoon freshly ground black pepper

½  cup milk

½  cup (4 ounces) sour cream

*Step into springtime with this bright, unique spinach and pea soup. Nutmeg and black pepper provide gentle seasoning, while sour cream adds smooth richness.*

Bring the water to a boil in a large saucepan over high heat. Add the peas. Cook, covered, for 1 minute. Stir in the broth, spinach, nutmeg, and pepper. Bring to a boil. Reduce the heat to low, cover, and simmer for 20 minutes. Let cool for 10 minutes.

Working in batches, puree the mixture in a blender or food processor. Return to the pan. Add the milk and sour cream and cook for 3 minutes, or until heated through.

**Makes 4 servings**

*Per serving: 144 calories, 8 g protein, 14 g carbohydrates, 7 g fat, 15 mg cholesterol, 5 g fiber, 502 mg sodium*

## COOKING TIP

Always add dairy products such as milk or sour cream to a soup or stew during the last few minutes of cooking. To prevent curdling, be sure to cook just until heated through but not to the boiling point.

# Cream of Tomato Soup

1 tablespoon olive oil

1 small onion, chopped

2 cups vegetable or chicken broth

1 can (14 ounces) diced tomatoes

1 teaspoon dried basil, crushed

¼ cup milk

Freshly ground black pepper

*Once you've tried this easy-to-make, fresh-tasting tomato soup, there's no going back to the canned variety. It pairs well with cornbread and a crisp salad.*

Heat the oil in a large saucepan over medium-high heat. Add the onion. Cook, stirring occasionally, for 5 minutes, or until soft. Add the broth, tomatoes (with juice), and basil. Bring to a boil. Reduce the heat to low, cover, and simmer for 20 minutes, or until slightly thickened. Let cool for 10 minutes.

Working in batches, puree the mixture in a blender or food processor. Return to the pan. Add the milk and cook 3 minutes or until heated through. Season with the pepper.

**Makes 4 servings**

*Per serving: 67 calories, 5 g protein, 7 g carbohydrates, 4 g fat, 3 mg cholesterol, 2 g fiber, 735 mg sodium*

### COOKING TIP

To get the most flavor from dried herbs, crush them before adding to the pan. To crush, simply place the desired amount of herbs in the palm of one hand and roll your other hand over them. Do this over the pan and sprinkle in when crushed.

# HEARTY
# MEAT
# STEWS

# Chili-Spiced Beef Stew

| 2 | tablespoons unbleached all-purpose flour |
|---|---|
| 4 | teaspoons chili powder |
| ½ | teaspoon salt |
| 2 | pounds beef stew meat |
| 1 | tablespoon olive oil |
| 2 | onions, sliced |
| 3 | cloves garlic, minced |
| 1 | teaspoon dried oregano |
| 2 | cups beef broth |
| 2 | cans (14 ounces each) stewed tomatoes |
| 1 | teaspoon sugar |
| ½ | teaspoon crushed red-pepper flakes |
| 2 | potatoes, cubed |
| 4 | carrots, sliced ½" thick |

*Braised beef spiked with red pepper, chili, and other seasonings makes this stew special. It freezes well, so you might want to simmer up a double batch.*

In a large resealable plastic bag, combine the flour, 1½ teaspoons of the chili powder, and the salt. Add the beef, seal the bag, and toss to coat well.

Heat the oil in a large saucepan over medium-high heat. Add the beef and cook, stirring occasionally, for 7 minutes, or until browned. Add the onions, garlic, and oregano. Reduce the heat to medium and cook, stirring often, for 5 minutes.

Add the broth, tomatoes, sugar, red-pepper flakes, and the remaining 2½ teaspoons chili powder. Bring to a boil. Reduce the heat to low, cover, and simmer for 2 hours, or until the beef is almost tender, stirring occasionally.

Add the potatoes and carrots. Cook, covered, for 30 minutes, or until the vegetables are tender.

### Makes 8 servings
*Per serving: 335 calories, 36 g protein, 23 g carbohydrates, 11 g fat, 88 mg cholesterol, 4 g fiber, 460 mg sodium*

# Beef Stew with Noodles

2 tablespoons olive oil

2 pounds beef stew meat

3 carrots, thinly sliced

2 onions, cut into wedges

4 cloves garlic, minced

2 tablespoons unbleached all-purpose flour

2 cups beef broth

2 cups water

½ cup red wine

1 teaspoon dried thyme leaves

½ pound green beans, cut into 1" pieces

1 teaspoon caraway seeds

16 ounces wide noodles, cooked

*Slow cooking tenderizes beef stew meat in this old favorite. Caraway seeds add a dash of fun and fresh flavor. Your family will love it.*

Heat the oil in a large saucepan over medium-high heat. Add the beef and cook, stirring often, for 7 minutes, or until brown. Add the carrots, onions, and garlic. Cook, stirring often, for 5 minutes, or until the vegetables are soft.

Add the flour and cook, stirring, for 2 minutes. Add the broth, water, wine, and thyme. Bring to a boil. Reduce the heat to low, cover, and simmer for 40 minutes.

Add the green beans and caraway seeds. Cook, covered, for 40 minutes, or until the stew is thick and the vegetables are tender.

Serve the stew over the hot cooked noodles.

### Makes 8 servings
*Per serving: 683 calories, 41 g protein, 48 g carbohydrates, 34 g fat, 183 mg cholesterol, 6 g fiber, 505 mg sodium*

# Southwest Beef Stew

2    tablespoons olive oil

2    pounds beef stew meat

1    large onion, thinly sliced

1    small jalapeño chile pepper, seeded and finely chopped (wear plastic gloves when handling)

3    cloves garlic, minced

3    tablespoons unbleached all-purpose flour

4    cups beef broth

1½    cups fresh or frozen and thawed corn

1    cup chopped roasted red peppers

1    large sweet potato, peeled and cubed

¾    teaspoon freshly ground black pepper

¼    cup chopped fresh cilantro

*This hearty winner gets its sizzle from a single jalapeño chile pepper. For less heat, but no less flavor, try an Anaheim chile. Serve the stew with a whole-grain bread and enjoy the combo for lunch or supper.*

Heat the oil in a large saucepan over medium-high heat. Add the beef and cook, stirring often, for 7 minutes, or until brown. Add the onion, jalapeño pepper, and garlic. Cook, stirring often, for 3 minutes. Stir in the flour and cook, stirring constantly, for 2 minutes.

Add the broth, corn, red peppers, sweet potato, and black pepper. Bring to a boil. Reduce the heat to low, cover, and simmer for 25 minutes, or until the stew is thick and the meat is tender. Stir in the cilantro.

### Makes 4 servings
*Per serving: 423 calories, 38 g protein, 30 g carbohydrates, 17 g fat, 88 mg cholesterol, 5 g fiber, 938 mg sodium*

# Beef and Black Bean Chili

1 tablespoon olive oil

1½ pounds lean ground beef

2 red onions, cut into thin wedges

3 cloves garlic, minced

1 can (14 ounces) crushed tomatoes

2 jalapeño chile peppers, seeded and chopped (wear plastic gloves when handling)

1 tablespoon chili powder

1 teaspoon dried oregano

¼ teaspoon celery seeds

1 teaspoon cumin seeds

½ teaspoon sugar

1 tomato, chopped

2 cans (15 ounces each) black beans, rinsed and drained

*Wake up your taste buds with this lively, classic chili. The snap comes from chili powder plus two chile peppers. The recipe comes together in no time flat, making it ideal for an impromptu gathering.*

Heat the oil in a large saucepan over medium-high heat. Add the beef and cook, stirring frequently, for 8 minutes, or until no longer pink. Add the onions and cook, stirring occasionally, for 5 minutes, or until soft. Add the garlic and cook for 1 minute.

Add the tomatoes, jalapeño peppers, chili powder, oregano, celery seeds, cumin seeds, and sugar. Bring to a boil. Reduce the heat to low, cover, and simmer for 10 minutes. Add the tomato and beans and cook 3 minutes to heat through.

**Makes 6 servings**
*Per serving: 373 calories, 42 g protein, 31 g carbohydrates, 11 g fat, 101 mg cholesterol, 10 g fiber, 486 mg sodium*

# Beef Burgundy

¼ cup unbleached all-purpose flour

¼ teaspoon salt

¼ teaspoon freshly ground black pepper

1½ pounds beef stew meat

2 tablespoons olive oil

½ pound pearl onions

1 pound mushrooms, quartered

3 cloves garlic, minced

3 cups burgundy wine

4 cups beef broth

¼ cup tomato paste

1 teaspoon cocoa

2 bay leaves

1 bunch baby carrots, halved

1 cup frozen peas, thawed

¼ cup chopped fresh Italian parsley

*This version of the classic French boeuf bourguignon is simple yet sophisticated. Beef, burgundy, onions, and mushrooms are the hallmarks of this favorite dish. Partner with an arugula-walnut-orange salad and a full-flavored red wine.*

In a resealable plastic bag, combine the flour, salt, and pepper. Add the beef, seal the bag, and toss to coat well.

Heat 1 tablespoon of the oil in a large saucepan over medium-high heat. Add the beef in batches to prevent overcrowding, and cook, stirring frequently, for 5 minutes, or until browned. Remove to a plate and repeat with remaining beef.

Add the remaining 1 tablespoon of oil to the pan. Add the onions, mushrooms, and garlic. Cook, stirring often, for 10 minutes, or until lightly browned.

Add the wine, broth, tomato paste, cocoa, bay leaves, and beef. Bring to a boil. Reduce the heat to low, cover, and simmer for 1½ hours.

Add the carrots and simmer, covered, for 40 minutes, or until the beef and vegetables are tender. Add the peas and cook for 5 minutes. Discard the bay leaves. Sprinkle with the parsley.

## Makes 8 servings
*Per serving: 381 calories, 32 g protein, 19 g carbohydrates, 12 g fat, 67 mg cholesterol, 4 g fiber, 524 mg sodium*

# Broccoli and Beef Stew

1/3 cup unbleached all-
purpose flour

1 teaspoon garlic powder

1/2 teaspoon freshly ground
black pepper

1/4 teaspoon salt

1 pound beef stew meat

2 tablespoons olive oil

1 onion, cut into thin
wedges

4 cups beef broth

3 large potatoes, cubed

1 teaspoon dried oregano

1/2 bunch broccoli, broken
into small florets (about
4 cups)

1/4 cup (2 ounces) grated
Parmesan cheese

*Some Parmesan cheese and just a smidgen of oregano take this simple stew from ordinary to extraordinary. For the freshest flavor, keep cooking time short after adding the broccoli.*

In a resealable plastic bag, combine the flour, garlic powder, pepper, and salt. Add the beef, seal the bag, and toss to coat well.

Heat the oil in a large saucepan over medium-high heat. Add the beef and cook, stirring occasionally, for 5 minutes, or until browned. Add the onion and cook, stirring occasionally, for 5 minutes, or until soft.

Add the broth, potatoes, and oregano. Bring to a boil. Reduce the heat to low, cover, and simmer for 20 minutes. Add the broccoli and cook for 5 minutes, or until the broccoli is tender-crisp.

Sprinkle with the cheese.

## Makes 4 servings

*Per serving: 633 calories, 42 g protein, 35 g carbohydrates, 38 g fat, 123 mg cholesterol, 7 g fiber, 779 mg sodium*

# Garlicky Pork Stew

1 tablespoon olive oil

1 pork tenderloin (about ¾ pound), cut into ¾" pieces

6 large cloves garlic, minced

3 carrots, sliced

2 ribs celery, thinly sliced

1 large onion, chopped

¼ cup unbleached all-purpose flour

4 cups chicken broth

3 large red potatoes, cubed

1 can (14½–19 ounces) red kidney beans, rinsed and drained

1 teaspoon ground sage

½ teaspoon freshly ground black pepper

¼ teaspoon salt

½ cup (4 ounces) sour cream

*This stew brings together pork and garlic—an irresistible pair. Toss in some carrots, potatoes, and beans for a stick-to-your-ribs dish that's a hit year-round.*

Heat the oil in a large saucepan over medium-high heat. Add the pork and cook, stirring occasionally, for 5 minutes. Add the garlic, carrots, celery, and onion. Cook for 3 minutes. Stir in the flour and cook, stirring, for 1 minute.

Add the broth, potatoes, beans, sage, pepper, and salt. Bring to a boil. Reduce the heat to low, cover, and simmer for 20 minutes, or until the stew is thick, the pork is no longer pink in the center, and the vegetables are tender.

Serve with the sour cream.

**Makes 6 servings**

*Per serving: 341 calories, 28 g protein, 40 g carbohydrates, 8 g fat, 52 mg cholesterol, 9 g fiber, 553 mg sodium*

# Savory Pork Stew

¼ cup unbleached all-purpose flour

½ teaspoon salt

½ teaspoon freshly ground black pepper

1 pound cubed pork loin

2 tablespoons olive oil

1 onion, chopped

6 cloves garlic, minced

2 cans (14 ounces each) diced tomatoes

2 tablespoons balsamic vinegar

2 carrots, sliced

1 red potato, cubed

2 teaspoons dried thyme leaves, crushed

*The surprise ingredient in this enticing stew is balsamic vinegar, a renowned Italian favorite that gets better and better with age and has a pungent-sweet flavor. This stew, though, is best enjoyed fresh. Accompany with buttery biscuits.*

In a resealable plastic bag, combine the flour, salt, and pepper. Add the pork, seal the bag, and toss to coat well.

Heat the olive oil in a large saucepan over medium-high heat. Add the pork and cook, stirring occasionally, for 5 minutes, or until browned. Add the onion and garlic and cook, stirring occasionally, for 3 minutes, or until golden.

Add the tomatoes (with juice), vinegar, carrots, potato, and thyme. Bring to a boil. Reduce the heat to low, cover, and simmer for 2 hours, or until the pork and vegetables are tender.

**4 servings**

*Per serving: 355 calories, 29 g protein, 29 g carbohydrates, 14 g fat, 67 mg cholesterol, 4 g fiber, 1,004 mg sodium*

# Thai Pork Stew

| | |
|---|---|
| 2 | tablespoons olive oil |
| 1 | pork tenderloin (about ¾ pound), cut into 1½" pieces |
| 2 | carrots, sliced |
| 2 | cloves garlic, minced |
| 1 | onion, cut into thin wedges |
| 1 | rib celery, thinly sliced |
| 6 | cups chicken broth |
| ¾ | cup basmati or long-grain rice |
| ½ | teaspoon Thai seasoning |
| ¼ | teaspoon salt |
| 4 | cups chopped green Swiss chard |
| 1½ | teaspoons grated lemon peel |
| 2½ | teaspoons lemon juice |

*Here, Thai seasoning—a charming blend of chile pepper, ginger, coriander, cumin, cinnamon, and star anise—teams with lots of lemon to bring pork tenderloin to perfection.*

Heat the oil in a large saucepan over medium-high heat. Add the pork and cook, stirring occasionally, for 5 minutes. Add the carrots, garlic, onion, and celery. Cook for 3 minutes.

Add the broth, rice, Thai seasoning, and salt. Bring to a boil. Reduce the heat to low, cover, and simmer for 30 minutes, or until the carrots and rice are tender.

Add the chard. Cook, covered, for 6 minutes, or until tender. Stir in the lemon peel and lemon juice.

**Makes 4 servings**
*Per serving: 463 calories, 38 g protein, 37 g carbohydrates, 18 g fat, 90 mg cholesterol, 5 g fiber, 892 mg sodium*

---

**COOKING TIP**

Be sure to use green Swiss chard in this dish. Red chard will turn the dish pink.

# Italian Sausage and White Bean Stew

1 large onion, sliced

1 green bell pepper, thinly sliced

1 pound hot Italian sausage, cut into 1" pieces

5 large cloves garlic, minced

2 carrots, chopped

⅓ cup unbleached all-purpose flour

3 cups chicken or vegetable broth

1 cup water

1 can (15 ounces) small white beans, rinsed and drained

1 teaspoon dried Italian herb seasoning

⅛ teaspoon crushed red-pepper flakes

8 ounces spinach, stems removed

*A perennial favorite—hot Italian sausage—perks up this stew of carrots, onions, peppers, spinach, and white beans. For different character, replace the hot sausage with the sweet variety.*

Coat a large nonstick saucepan with cooking spray. Heat over medium heat. Add the onion, bell pepper, and sausage. Cook, stirring occasionally, for 10 minutes, or until the onion and sausage are lightly browned. Add the garlic, carrots, and flour. Cook for 1 minute.

Add the broth, water, beans, Italian herb seasoning, and red-pepper flakes. Bring to a boil. Reduce the heat to low, cover, and simmer for 30 minutes, or until the stew is thick and the sausage is no longer pink. Stir in the spinach. Cook for 1 minute, or until the spinach has wilted.

**Makes 6 servings**

*Per serving: 402 calories, 19 g protein, 32 g carbohydrates, 24 g fat, 60 mg cholesterol, 12 g fiber, 1,006 mg sodium*

# Lamb and Rice Stew

1    **cup basmati or long-grain rice**

1    **tablespoon olive oil**

1    **pound cubed lamb**

2    **cans (14 ounces each) stewed tomatoes, cut into pieces**

¼    **cup dry red wine**

4    **cloves garlic, minced**

2    **teaspoons dried chives**

1    **teaspoon dried rosemary, crushed**

1    **teaspoon dried Italian seasoning**

½    **teaspoon hot-pepper sauce**

*Rosemary and lamb always make a natural and tasty pair. Here, the delightful duo appears with stewed tomatoes and long-grain basmati rice, which can be found in large supermarkets as well as specialty groceries.*

Prepare the rice according to package directions.

Meanwhile, heat the oil in a large saucepan over medium-high heat. Add the lamb and cook, stirring occasionally, for 5 minutes, or until browned.

Add the tomatoes (with juice), wine, garlic, chives, rosemary, and Italian seasoning. Bring to a boil. Reduce the heat to low, cover, and simmer for 15 minutes, or until the lamb is tender. Add the hot-pepper sauce. Serve over the rice.

**Makes 4 servings**

*Per serving: 479 calories, 27 g protein, 46 g carbohydrates, 20 g fat, 82 mg cholesterol, 5 g fiber, 676 mg sodium*

---

**COOKING TIP**

Pepper sauces come in all degrees of heat, ranging from mild, such as Crystal's, to searingly hot, such as Tabasco. Add mild sauces to recipes by the teaspoonfuls. Add hot sauces to recipes by the drop.

# Moroccan Lamb Stew

1 tablespoon unbleached all-purpose flour

1 tablespoon curry powder

¼ teaspoon salt

1 pound cubed lamb

1 tablespoon olive oil

2 cups chicken broth

2 carrots, chopped

1 onion, chopped

1 red potato, cubed

1 small head cauliflower, cut into florets

¼ cup chopped dried apricots

¼ teaspoon ground cinnamon

¼ teaspoon crushed red-pepper flakes

¼ teaspoon grated lemon peel

1 cup couscous

*Reward yourself with this captivating yet easy North African master-piece. In it, the flavors of apricots, cinnamon, and curry intermingle to satisfy the most discriminating palate.*

In a resealable plastic bag, combine the flour, curry powder, and salt. Add the lamb, seal the bag, and toss to coat well.

Heat the oil in a large saucepan over medium-high heat. Add the lamb and cook, stirring occasionally, for 5 minutes. Gradually add the broth, stirring constantly. Cook for 5 minutes, stirring frequently.

Add the carrots, onion, potato, cauliflower, apricots, cinnamon, red-pepper flakes, and lemon peel. Bring to a boil. Reduce the heat to low, cover, and simmer for 40 minutes, or until the stew is thick and the potatoes and carrots are tender.

Meanwhile, prepare the couscous according to package directions. Serve topped with the stew.

### Makes 4 servings
*Per serving: 552 calories, 35 g protein, 60 g carbohydrates, 20 g fat, 82 mg cholesterol, 11 g fiber, 605 mg sodium*

# FAVORITE FISH STEWS

# Bouillabaisse with Herbed Toast

1   tablespoon olive oil

1   onion, chopped

4   scallions, thinly sliced

5   cloves garlic, minced

2   small red potatoes, quartered

2   bottles (8 ounces each) clam juice

1   can (28 ounces) diced tomatoes

1   cup dry white wine

1   pound cod, cubed

8   ounces sea scallops

8   ounces large shrimp, peeled and deveined

1   tablespoon chopped fresh dill

1   tablespoon chopped fresh basil

Salt

Pinch of ground red pepper

8   slices French bread

1   tablespoon olive oil

1   tablespoon dried marjoram

1   teaspoon garlic powder

1   tablespoon (½ ounce) grated Romano cheese

*The very essence of Provence, this superb bouillabaisse has all the tempting flavors for a winter evening's feast. Serve it in big crockery bowls with a tossed salad.*

Preheat the oven to 400°F.

Heat the oil in a large saucepan over medium-high heat. Add the onion, scallions, garlic, and potatoes. Cook, stirring often, for 5 minutes, or until soft. Add the clam juice, tomatoes (with juice), and wine. Bring to a boil. Reduce the heat to low, cover, and simmer, stirring occasionally, for 10 minutes.

Add the cod, scallops, and shrimp. Cook, stirring occasionally, for 5 minutes, or until the fish, scallops, and shrimp are opaque. Add the dill and basil. Season with salt and pepper.

Arrange the bread on a large baking sheet. Brush each slice with the oil. Sprinkle the marjoram, garlic powder, and cheese over each slice. Bake for 15 minutes, or until crisp and golden brown. Serve with the stew.

**Makes 6 servings**

*Per serving: 360 calories, 32 g protein, 32 g carbohydrates, 8 g fat, 103 mg cholesterol, 3 g fiber, 896 mg sodium*

# Santa Fe Seafood Stew

2 tablespoons olive oil

2 onions, chopped

2 cloves garlic, minced

1 teaspoon chili powder

6 cups chicken broth

2 russet potatoes, cubed

1 chipotle chile pepper, seeded and minced

1 pound sea scallops

2 cups fresh or frozen and thawed corn kernels

¾ cup chopped roasted sweet red peppers

¼ cup unbleached all-purpose flour

2 cups milk

½ cup chopped fresh cilantro

*Ready for an intriguing Southwest spin on seafood? It's here in this colorful dish. Chipotle pepper—a dried, smoked jalapeño—adds the magical hint of sweet-spicy, almost chocolate flavor.*

Heat the oil in a large saucepan over medium-high heat. Add the onions, garlic, and chili powder. Cook, stirring often, for 5 minutes, or until the onions are soft.

Add the broth, potatoes, and chile pepper. Bring to a boil. Reduce the heat to low, cover, and simmer for 15 minutes. Add the scallops, corn, and roasted peppers. Simmer, covered, for 10 minutes, or until the potatoes are tender and the scallops are opaque.

In a medium bowl, whisk together the milk and flour. Add to the soup. Cook, stirring often, for 3 minutes, or until slightly thickened. Stir in the cilantro.

**Makes 8 servings**

*Per serving: 211 calories, 15 g protein, 24 g carbohydrates, 7 g fat, 23 mg cholesterol, 3 g fiber, 879 mg sodium*

## COOKING TIP

Chipotle peppers are smoke-dried jalapeño peppers. Some supermarkets carry them in the produce section. They can also be found canned in adobo sauce in the international aisle of many large supermarkets.

# Easy Oyster Stew

1 tablespoon olive oil
1 onion, finely chopped
1 clove garlic, minced
½ teaspoon dried marjoram
¼ teaspoon celery seeds
1 potato, cubed
2 cups chicken broth
1 bottle (8 ounces) clam juice
1 cup frozen corn, thawed
¾ pound small shucked oysters, rinsed and drained
1 cup milk
⅓ cup crushed saltine crackers
2 tablespoons finely chopped fresh parsley

*Oysters have been a mainstay of fine dining since the nineteenth century, a tradition that holds to this day. Ready in just 30 minutes, this stew is fit for a feast.*

Heat the oil in a large saucepan over medium-high heat. Add the onion and cook, stirring occasionally, for 5 minutes, or until soft. Add the garlic, marjoram, and celery seeds. Cook, stirring, for 1 minute.

Add the potato, broth, and clam juice. Bring to a boil. Reduce the heat to low, cover, and simmer for 15 minutes, or until the potatoes are tender.

Add the corn and oysters. Simmer, covered, for 5 minutes, or until the oysters are just cooked through and their edges have begun to curl. Add the milk, crackers, and parsley. Cook 2 minutes or until slightly thickened.

**Makes 4 servings**
*Per serving: 273 calories, 12 g protein, 37 g carbohydrates, 9 g fat, 49 mg cholesterol, 3 g fiber, 885 mg sodium*

# Southwest Shrimp Stew

1    potato, peeled and cubed

2    cups chicken broth

1    tablespoon olive oil

2    scallions, thinly sliced

1    small red bell pepper, chopped

1    small green bell pepper, chopped

2    cups frozen corn, thawed

1    teaspoon cumin seeds

¼    teaspoon salt

2    cups milk

¾    pound small shrimp, peeled and deveined

    Dash of ground red pepper

¼    cup chopped fresh cilantro leaves

*Peppers, corn, and other favorite vegetables create a riot of color in this Tex-Mex-seasoned stew. It's company-friendly but easy enough for every day.*

Cook the potato in water in a medium covered saucepan for 15 minutes, or until tender. Drain. Add 1 cup of the broth. Mash with a fork, potato masher, or hand-held immersion blender until free of lumps.

Heat the oil in a large saucepan over medium-high heat. Add the scallions and bell peppers. Cook, stirring frequently, for 5 minutes, or until the vegetables are soft.

Add corn, cumin seeds, salt, potato mixture, and remaining 1 cup broth. Bring to a boil. Reduce the heat to low, cover, and simmer for 5 minutes. Add the milk and return to a simmer. Add the shrimp and simmer, stirring occasionally, for 1 to 2 minutes, or until opaque. Stir in the ground red pepper and cilantro.

**Makes 8 servings**

*Per serving: 148 calories, 13 g protein, 17 g carbohydrates, 4 g fat, 69 mg cholesterol, 2 g fiber, 314 mg sodium*

# Seafood Gumbo

2    **cups basmati rice**

2    **tablespoons olive oil**

1    **tablespoon unbleached all-purpose flour**

2    **onions, chopped**

1    **green bell pepper, chopped**

1    **rib celery, thinly sliced**

3    **cans (14 ounces each) stewed tomatoes**

1    **cup sliced okra**

½    **pound haddock, cut into 1" cubes**

½    **pound medium shrimp, peeled and deveined**

½    **pound sea scallops**

¼    **pound shucked oysters, drained and rinsed**

1    **teaspoon hot-pepper sauce**

½    **teaspoon filé powder**

*Genuine Creole influences abound in this hearty gumbo courtesy of okra, filé, and the favored Louisiana trio: peppers, onions, and celery.*

Prepare the rice according to package directions.

Meanwhile, in a large saucepan, combine the oil and flour. Cook over medium heat for 3 to 5 minutes, stirring constantly, until the mixture turns dark brown. Add the onions, bell pepper, and celery. Cook, stirring, for 3 to 4 minutes, or until the vegetables begin to soften.

Add the tomatoes and okra and bring to a boil. Reduce the heat to low, cover, and simmer for 5 minutes. Add the haddock, shrimp, scallops, and oysters. Simmer, covered, for 5 minutes, or until the fish, shrimp, scallops, and oysters are opaque. Remove from the heat and stir in the hot-pepper sauce and filé powder.

Serve over the hot rice.

**Makes 8 servings**

*Per serving: 367 calories, 22 g protein, 53 g carbohydrates, 7 g fat, 74 mg cholesterol, 4 g fiber, 703 mg sodium*

---

**COOKING TIP**

Filé (fee-lay) powder is a Creole seasoning made from the dried leaves of the sassafras tree and imparts a flavor similar to root beer. It is available in the spice section of almost any large supermarket. It should be added to a dish when it has been removed from the heat or the filé will become tough and stringy.

# Haddock Stew
# with Shallots and Dill

| | |
|---|---|
| 2 | tablespoons olive oil |
| 5 | shallots, thinly sliced |
| 2 | cups chicken broth |
| 2 | potatoes, cut into ½" cubes |
| 2 | carrots, thinly sliced |
| ½ | teaspoon dry mustard |
| ¼ | teaspoon celery seeds |
| ½ | teaspoon salt |
| ¼ | teaspoon ground white pepper |
| 1 | pound skinless haddock fillet, cut into 2" pieces |
| 1 | cup milk |
| ¼ | cup finely chopped fresh dill |
| 2 | tablespoons finely chopped fresh parsley |

*Sporting a mild-flavored white fish and light seasonings, this stew is sure to be a family favorite. Serve with hot corn bread or cheese biscuits.*

Heat the oil in a large saucepan over medium-high heat. Add the shallots and cook, stirring occasionally, for 5 minutes, or just until soft. Add the broth, potatoes, carrots, mustard, celery seeds, salt, and pepper. Bring to a boil. Reduce the heat to low, cover, and simmer for 15 minutes, or until the vegetables are tender.

Add the haddock. Simmer, covered, for 5 minutes, or until the fish is opaque. Stir in the milk, dill, and parsley. Simmer for 3 minutes, or until heated through.

**Makes 4 servings**
*Per serving: 286 calories, 27 g protein, 22 g carbohydrates, 10 g fat, 69 mg cholesterol, 3 g fiber, 557 mg sodium*

---

**COOKING TIP**

To remove small bones from fish such as haddock, cod, or salmon, use needle-nose pliers.

# PERFECT POULTRY STEWS

# Chicken Stew Provençal

2 tablespoons olive oil

4 chicken legs, cut into thighs and drumsticks, skinned

2 large onions, sliced into thin wedges

2 large ribs celery, sliced

4 large cloves garlic, minced

2 cups chicken broth

1 can (14 ounces) whole tomatoes, cut up

4 red potatoes, cut into 1" chunks

2 teaspoons dried herbs de Provence

½ teaspoon salt

½ teaspoon freshly ground black pepper

*Herbs de Provence—a blend of seven favored French herbs including marjoram, lavender, and fennel—imparts the tantalizing aromas of French countryside cooking to this superb stew. Serve with a crusty farm-style bread for sopping up the light broth.*

Heat the oil in a large saucepan over medium-high heat. Add the chicken and cook, turning occasionally, for 10 minutes, or until browned on all sides. Add the onions, celery, and garlic. Cook, stirring occasionally, for 5 minutes, or until the onions are lightly browned.

Add the broth, tomatoes (with juice), potatoes, herbs de Provence, salt, and pepper. Bring to a boil. Reduce the heat to low, cover, and simmer for 45 minutes, or until the chicken is no longer pink and the potatoes are tender.

**Makes 4 servings**

*Per serving: 295 calories, 18 g protein, 35 g carbohydrates, 10 g fat, 41 mg cholesterol, 5 g fiber, 786 mg sodium*

## COOKING TIP

Herbs de Provence is a blend of the most commonly used dried herbs in southern French cooking. It commonly includes rosemary, marjoram, thyme, sage, fennel seed, lavender, and summer savory. The blend can be found in the spice aisle of most supermarkets. If it's unavailable, use a combination of any three of these.

# Ragoût of Chicken and Tomato

4  chicken breast halves, skinned

¼  teaspoon salt

¼  teaspoon freshly ground black pepper

1  tablespoon olive oil

2  carrots, thinly sliced

1  onion, chopped

1  cup chicken broth

1  can (28 ounces) diced tomatoes

½  cup dry white wine

¼  teaspoon fennel seeds, crushed

1  head cauliflower, cut into florets

1  large fennel bulb, sliced

2  teaspoons minced fresh or dried chives

8  ounces medium noodles, cooked

*Imagine dining in a French bistro and savoring tender, succulent chicken in a well-seasoned ragoût (stew) of fresh vegetables.*

Season the chicken with the salt and pepper. Heat the oil in a large saucepan over medium-high heat. Add the chicken and cook for 5 minutes, or until lightly browned. Turn breasts and move to the sides of the pan. Add the carrots and onion. Cook, stirring frequently, for 5 minutes.

Add the broth, tomatoes (with juice), wine, and fennel seed. Bring to a boil. Reduce the heat to low, cover, and simmer for 20 minutes, or until a thermometer inserted in the thickest portion of the chicken registers 170°F and the juices run clear. Add the cauliflower, fennel, and chives. Simmer, covered, for 7 minutes, or until the vegetables are tender. Serve over the hot noodles.

**Makes 4 servings**

*Per serving: 585 calories, 50 g protein, 74 g carbohydrates, 11 g fat, 142 mg cholesterol, 14 g fiber, 774 mg sodium*

# Easy Chicken Stew
# with Parsley Dumplings

## Stew

| | |
|---|---|
| 2 | tablespoons olive oil |
| 1 | pound boneless, skinless chicken breast, cut into 1" pieces |
| 1 | onion, chopped |
| 1 | rib celery, chopped |
| 2 | tablespoons unbleached all-purpose flour |
| 4 | cups chicken broth |
| 1 | teaspoon poultry seasoning |
| ⅛ | teaspoon freshly ground black pepper |
| 2 | carrots, thinly sliced |
| 1 | bunch broccoli, cut into florets |

## Dumplings

| | |
|---|---|
| 1 | cup unbleached all-purpose flour |
| 1½ | teaspoons sugar |
| ¾ | teaspoon baking powder |
| ¼ | teaspoon salt |
| 2 | tablespoons cold butter, cut into small pieces |
| ¾ | cup buttermilk |
| 2 | teaspoons parsley |

*When's the last time you had tender dumplings like those mom used to make? Wait no longer. These light and fuss-free dumplings make great comfort food, too.*

*To make the stew:* Heat the oil in a large saucepan over medium-high heat. Add the chicken and cook, stirring frequently, for 5 minutes, or until lightly browned. Add the onion and celery. Cook for 5 minutes, or until tender. Add the flour and cook for 2 minutes.

Gradually add the broth, stirring constantly. Add the poultry seasoning and pepper. Bring to a boil. Reduce the heat to low, cover, and simmer for 15 minutes. Add the carrots and broccoli.

*To make the dumplings:* In a medium bowl, combine the flour, sugar, baking powder, and salt. Using a pastry blender, cut the butter into the flour mixture until coarse crumbs form.

Add the buttermilk and parsley. Using a fork, stir until just moistened. Ater adding the carrots and broccoli to the stew, remove from the heat and drop the dumplings by the tablespoonfuls on top of the chicken mixture.

Return the pan to the heat. Simmer, covered, for 12 to 15 minutes, or until a wooden pick inserted into the center of a dumpling comes out clean.

**Makes 4 servings**
*Per serving: 487 calories, 41 g protein, 40 g carbohydrates, 18 g fat, 97 mg cholesterol, 3 g fiber, 971 mg sodium*

# Chicken Potpie

## Potpie

2    tablespoons olive oil

1    pound boneless, skinless chicken breast, cut into 1" pieces

1    russet potato, cubed

1    carrot, thinly sliced

2    cups chicken broth

¾    cup pearl onions

1    cup fresh or frozen and thawed snow peas

1    teaspoon dried thyme leaves

¼    teaspoon freshly ground black pepper

1    tablespoon quick-cooking tapioca

## Biscuits

1    cup unbleached all-purpose flour

2    teaspoons baking powder

¼    teaspoon salt

½    cup buttermilk

¼    cup olive oil

*The first frozen chicken potpie debuted in 1951, and dining hasn't been the same since. This fresh-ingredient version, though, beats the frozen variety hands down every time.*

Preheat the oven to 425°F. Coat a 2-quart baking dish with cooking spray. Set aside.

*To make the potpie:* Heat the oil in a large saucepan over medium-high heat. Add the chicken and cook, stirring occasionally, for 5 minutes, or until lightly browned. Add the potato, carrot, and broth. Bring to a boil. Reduce the heat to low, cover, and simmer for 10 minutes. Add the onions, peas, thyme, pepper, and tapioca. Place in the baking dish.

*To make the biscuits:* In a large bowl, combine the flour, baking powder, and salt. In a small bowl, mix the buttermilk and oil. Mix into the flour mixture until just moistened. Spoon 8 mounds onto the chicken mixture. Bake for 20 minutes, or until golden and a wooden pick inserted into the center of a biscuit comes out clean.

### Makes 8 servings

*Per serving: 251 calories, 14 g protein, 23 g carbohydrates, 11 g fat, 25 mg cholesterol, 2 g fiber, 393 mg sodium*

# Chicken Stew with Butternut Squash

1    **cup wild rice**

1    **tablespoon olive oil**

1    **pound boneless, skinless chicken breast, cut into 1" pieces**

2    **large onions, cut into wedges**

8    **ounces mushrooms, sliced**

2    **cloves garlic, minced**

2    **cups chicken broth**

2    **cups apple cider or juice**

1    **small butternut squash, peeled, seeded, and cut into 1" pieces**

½    **teaspoon five-spice powder**

3    **tablespoons water**

2    **tablespoons cornstarch**

*Dine on the wild side—sort of. This savory dish features wild rice and brings apple cider, five-spice powder, chicken, and winter squash together in an earthy combination that will satisfy the heartiest of appetites.*

Cook the rice according to package directions.

Meanwhile, heat the oil in a large saucepan over medium-high heat. Add the chicken and cook, stirring occasionally, for 5 minutes, or until lightly browned. Add the onions and mush-rooms. Cook for 5 minutes. Add the garlic and cook for 1 minute.

Add the broth, cider, squash, and five-spice powder. Bring to a boil. Reduce the heat to low, cover, and simmer for 25 min-utes, or until the squash is tender.

In a cup, combine the water and cornstarch. Gradually add to the chicken mixture. Cook, stirring, for 2 minutes, or until thickened. Serve over the rice.

**Makes 4 servings**

*Per serving: 474 calories, 36 g protein, 71 g carbohydrates, 7 g fat, 66 mg cholesterol, 7 g fiber, 376 mg sodium*

### COOKING TIP

An easy way to cut through winter squash shells is to first cook the squash in a microwave oven. Simply cook on high for 5 minutes and the knife will slide right through the shell.

# Spring Chicken Stew

1   **pound boneless, skinless chicken breasts, cut into 1" strips**

4   **cups chicken broth**

3   **carrots, sliced ½" thick**

2   **red potatoes, quartered**

2   **cloves garlic, minced**

1   **teaspoon dried thyme leaves, crushed**

1   **teaspoon dried basil**

1   **medium zucchini, sliced**

¼   **pound asparagus, diagonally sliced into 1" pieces**

2   **tablespoons unbleached all-purpose flour**

¼   **cup milk**

3   **tablespoons parsley**

¼   **teaspoon ground white pepper**

*Here's a delectable stew with spring and summer vegetables—asparagus, zucchini, and red potatoes. It's sure to earn five stars in your recipe collection.*

In a large saucepan, combine the chicken, broth, carrots, potatoes, garlic, thyme, and basil. Bring to a boil. Reduce the heat to low, cover, and simmer for 15 minutes, or until the chicken is no longer pink and the vegetables are tender. Skim foam from the surface as necessary. Add the zucchini and asparagus. Cook for 2 minutes, or until just tender.

In a small bowl, whisk together the flour, milk, parsley, and pepper. Gradually add to the chicken mixture and cook 2 minutes, or until thickened.

**Makes 4 servings**
*Per serving: 238 calories, 31 g protein, 24 g carbohydrates, 2 g fat, 66 mg cholesterol, 4 g fiber, 680 mg sodium*

---

**COOKING TIP**

Parsley comes in two varieties—flat-leaf and curly leaf. The flat-leaf variety has slightly more flavor.

# Tomato-Turkey Stew with Gremolata

## Stew

2    tablespoons olive oil

6    scallions, chopped

2    carrots, chopped

2    cloves garlic, minced

1    rib celery, thinly sliced

1    tablespoon grated lemon peel

1    pound boneless, skinless turkey breast, cut into 1" cubes

1    can (14 ounces) diced tomatoes

1    cup white wine

    Juice of 1 lemon

1    teaspoon dried Italian herb seasoning

½    teaspoon salt

¼    teaspoon freshly ground black pepper

## Gremolata

1    tablespoon finely chopped fresh parsley

1    teaspoon grated lemon peel

1    clove garlic, minced

1    teaspoon salt

*This lemony Milanese stew is served with gremolata, a lively mixture of garlic, parsley, and lemon peel. If you prefer, chicken or pork can replace the turkey.*

*To make the stew:* Heat the oil in a large saucepan over medium-high heat. Add the scallions, carrots, garlic, celery, and lemon peel. Cook, stirring frequently, for 2 minutes. Add the turkey and cook, stirring, for 10 minutes, or until lightly browned.

Add the tomatoes (with juice), wine, lemon juice, Italian herb seasoning, salt, and pepper. Bring to boil. Reduce the heat to low, cover, and simmer for 10 minutes. Uncover and simmer for 10 minutes, or until the sauce thickens.

*To make the gremolata:* In a small bowl, combine the parsley, lemon peel, garlic, and salt. Sprinkle over each serving of the turkey mixture.

### Makes 4 servings

*Per serving: 307 calories, 36 g protein, 14 g carbohydrates, 8 g fat, 94 mg cholesterol, 5 g fiber, 773 mg sodium*

# Turkey Stew with Biscuit Crust

## Biscuits

1  cup unbleached all-purpose flour
1  teaspoon baking powder
¼  teaspoon baking soda
¼  teaspoon salt
2  tablespoons cold butter, cut into small pieces
¼  cup buttermilk
3  tablespoons sour cream

## Stew

1  tablespoon olive oil
2  cloves garlic, minced
1  small onion, chopped
2½  teaspoons cornstarch
1  teaspoon dried thyme leaves, crushed
½  teaspoon rubbed sage
2  cups chicken broth
1  cup fresh or frozen and thawed peas
2  carrots, very thinly sliced
1  small head cauliflower, cut into small florets
2  cups skinless cooked turkey, cubed
¼  teaspoon freshly ground black pepper

*Sometimes, old-fashioned is best—especially when it comes to stews. This turkey version is bursting with vegetables and sports a simple, home-style biscuit crust. Your family is sure to love it.*

Preheat the oven to 425°F. Coat a 2-quart baking dish with cooking spray. Set aside.

*To make the biscuits:* In a medium bowl, combine the flour, baking powder, baking soda, and salt. Using a pastry blender, cut in the butter until the mixture forms crumbs. Add the buttermilk and sour cream. Mix and gather into a ball. Turn onto a sheet of plastic wrap and flatten into a round. Wrap and refrigerate.

*To make the stew:* Heat the oil in a large saucepan over medium-high heat. Add the garlic and onion. Cook, stirring occasionally, for 2 minutes.

In a medium bowl, combine the cornstarch, thyme, and sage. Whisk in the broth. Add to the onion mixture. Bring to a boil and cook, stirring, for 1 minute or until thickened. Remove from the heat. Add the peas, carrots, cauliflower, turkey, and pepper. Place in the prepared baking dish.

Cut the biscuit dough into 4 equal parts. Arrange on the turkey mixture.

Bake for 30 minutes, or until the biscuits are golden and the stew is bubbling.

**Makes 4 servings**
*Per serving: 419 calories, 38 g protein, 45 g carbohydrates, 11 g fat, 85 mg cholesterol, 10 g fiber, 826 mg sodium*

# Turkey, Rice, and Bean Stew

2    tablespoons olive oil
1    onion, chopped
1    pound turkey tenderloin, sliced into 1" pieces
5    cups chicken broth
1    cup brown rice
1    can (15 ounces) pinto beans, rinsed and drained
1    teaspoon cumin seeds, crushed
1    teaspoon oregano
1    pound spinach, coarsely chopped

*There's nothing retiring about this robust stew. In fact, it's bursting with hearty foods like brown rice and pinto beans. Aromatic cumin gives the broth a complex, nutty flavor.*

Heat the oil in a large saucepan over medium-high heat. Add the onion and turkey. Cook, stirring occasionally, for 10 minutes, or until the turkey is light brown.

Add the broth, rice, beans, cumin seeds, and oregano. Bring to a boil. Reduce the heat to low, cover, and simmer for 40 minutes, or until the rice is tender.

Add the spinach and cook for 2 minutes, or until wilted.

**Makes 4 servings**

*Per serving: 570 calories, 48 g protein, 66 g carbohydrates, 13 g fat, 79 mg cholesterol, 13 g fiber, 811 mg sodium*

---

**COOKING TIP**

Brown rice, like white rice, comes in many varieties. The most common is the long-grain variety. Try a short-grain brown rice in this and similar recipes. Short-grain rice is a bit firmer and chewier than its long-grain cousin.

# ON THE
# SIDE

# Garlic Bread with Asiago Cheese

2 bulbs garlic

¼ cup olive oil

1 loaf Italian bread, cut in half lengthwise

¼ cup (2 ounces) grated Asiago cheese

Paprika

*Here, an all-time favorite—garlic bread—gets a new spin. Garlic is roasted until it's buttery smooth and sweet, then spread over bread and topped with Asiago cheese.*

Preheat the oven to 350°F. Slice the top ¼" from each garlic bulb. Discard the tops. Lightly brush the bulbs with 1 table-spoon of the oil. Place in a shallow baking dish. Cover with foil.

Bake for 55 to 60 minutes. Remove the foil and bake for 10 minutes, or until the garlic skin is browned and the interior is very soft. Let cool for several minutes. When the bulbs are cool enough to handle, squeeze the cloves into a bowl and mash with a fork. Discard the skin. Add the remaining 3 tablespoons oil. Mash until smooth.

Preheat the broiler. Brush the garlic mixture over the bread halves. Sprinkle the cheese and paprika over the slices. Broil until golden. Cut into 16 slices.

**Makes 16 servings**

*Per serving: 135 calories, 4 g protein, 19 g carbohydrates, 5 g fat, 2 mg cholesterol, 1 g fiber, 206 mg sodium*

---

**COOKING TIP**

When young, Asiago—a popular Italian cheese with a rich, nutty flavor—makes a nice slicing cheese. When aged more than a year, Asiago is perfect for grating. Most Asiagos sold in the U.S. are grating cheeses.

# Rosemary Biscuits

2 cups unbleached all-purpose flour

1 teaspoon dried rosemary, crushed

2½ teaspoons baking powder

½ teaspoon baking soda

¼ teaspoon salt

4 tablespoons butter

⅔ cup buttermilk

*These tender, flaky biscuits pair perfectly with any of the soups and stews in this book. Rosemary's lemony-pine flavor is distinctive and assertive. If it's not for you, dill or parsley would substitute nicely.*

Preheat the oven to 425°F. Grease a baking sheet.

In a bowl, combine the flour, rosemary, baking powder, baking soda, and salt. Using a pastry blender, cut in 3 tablespoons of the butter until coarse crumbs form. Stir in the buttermilk until a dough forms.

Turn the dough out onto a lightly floured surface and knead for 1 minute.

Using a floured rolling pin, gently roll the dough into a ½"-thick rectangle, or flour your hands and pat into shape. Using a 2" biscuit cutter, cut the dough into rounds, rerolling as necessary to cut 16 biscuits.

Place the biscuits on the prepared baking sheet. Melt the remaining tablespoon of butter. Brush over the biscuits. Bake for 12 to 15 minutes, or until golden.

**Makes 16 servings**

*Per serving: 86 calories, 3 g protein, 14 g carbohydrates, 3 g fat, 7 mg cholesterol, 1 g fiber, 172 mg sodium*

# Olive-Caper Focaccia

1 package (¼ ounce) quick-rising yeast

1 cup warm water (105°–115°F)

1 teaspoon honey

3 cups unbleached all-purpose flour

3 tablespoons olive oil

¼ cup kalamata olives, pitted and chopped

2 teaspoons drained capers, chopped

1 tablespoon chopped fresh basil

1 tablespoon chopped fresh thyme

1½ teaspoons salt

*What could be more typical of Mediterranean cross-border cuisine than a focaccia (Italian) bread laced with capers (French and sometimes Italian) and kalamata olives (Greek). But don't spend too much time pondering this fact—simply bake and enjoy!*

Preheat the oven to 400°F. Grease a baking sheet.

In a large mixing bowl, dissolve the yeast in the water. Stir in the honey and let stand for 5 minutes, or until the yeast is foamy. Add 1 cup of the flour. Beat with a wire whisk until smooth and creamy. Let rest at room temperature for 5 minutes.

Add 2 tablespoons of the oil, the olives, capers, basil, thyme, salt, and 1 cup of the remaining flour. Whisk hard for 3 minutes, or until smooth. Add the remaining ½ to 1 cup flour, a little at a time, beating with a wooden spoon until a soft, sticky dough forms.

Turn out onto a lightly floured surface and knead for 3 minutes.

Place on the prepared baking sheet and shape into a 12" round. Brush with the remaining 1 tablespoon oil.

Bake for 25 minutes, or until golden brown. Let cool on a rack for 5 minutes before serving.

**Makes 8 servings**

*Per serving: 87 calories, 6 g protein, 33 g carbohydrates, 7 g fat, 0 mg cholesterol, 1 g fiber, 501 mg sodium*

# Sun-Dried Tomato Semolina Bread

| | |
|---|---|
| 8 | dry-packed, sun-dried tomatoes, chopped |
| 1 | cup boiling water |
| 1 | tablespoon cornmeal |
| 1 | cup semolina flour |
| ½–¾ | cup unbleached flour |
| ½ | cup cornmeal |
| 2 | teaspoons baking powder |
| 2 | teaspoons dried oregano |
| 2 | teaspoons chopped fresh basil |
| ½ | teaspoon baking soda |
| ½ | teaspoon salt |
| 1 | cup tomato juice |
| 2 | tablespoons olive oil |

*Win accolades with this West Coast–style artisan bread that's loaded with tomato and fresh basil flavor. Warm from the oven, its aromas are tantalizing and its flavors are captivating.*

Soak the tomatoes in the boiling water for 5 minutes, or until softened. Drain. Preheat the oven to 400°F. Grease a 9" round baking pan. Dust the interior with the cornmeal.

In a food processor fitted with a steel blade, combine the semolina flour, ½ cup of the unbleached flour, the cornmeal, baking powder, oregano, basil, baking soda, and salt. Pulse for 20 seconds to combine.

Add the drained tomatoes, the tomato juice, and oil. Pulse a few seconds to form a dough, adding enough of the remaining unbleached flour to form a soft, moist dough.

With lightly floured hands, press the dough into the pan. Bake for 30 minutes, or until a wooden pick inserted in the center comes out clean. Let cool on a rack for 5 minutes before serving.

**Makes 10 servings**
*Per serving: 135 calories, 4 g protein, 24 g carbohydrates, 5 g fat, 0 mg cholesterol, 3 g fiber, 365 mg sodium*

# Caraway-Pepper Soda Bread

1¾ cups whole-wheat flour

1½ cups unbleached all-purpose flour

2 tablespoons brown sugar

1 tablespoon caraway seeds

2 teaspoons baking powder

1 teaspoon baking soda

1 teaspoon cracked black pepper

¾ teaspoon salt

1½ cups buttermilk

2 tablespoons canola oil

*This quick bread gets its rising power—and its name—from baking soda. This recipe was inspired by Irish soda bread, which typically is made with currants, caraway seeds, and buttermilk.*

Preheat the oven to 400°F. Grease a 9" round cake pan.

In a food processor fitted with a steel blade, mix the whole-wheat flour, unbleached flour, brown sugar, caraway seeds, baking powder, baking soda, pepper, and salt. Add 1¼ cups of the buttermilk and the oil. Pulse to form a wet dough, adding the remaining ¼ cup buttermilk if the dough is too dry.

Place on a floured surface. Knead 10 times to form a round loaf. Cover lightly with flour. Press into the prepared pan. Cut an X into the center. Bake for 30 minutes, or until the bread is browned and shrinks from the sides of the pan. Let cool on a rack for 5 minutes before serving.

**Makes 8 servings**

*Per serving: 241 calories, 9 g protein, 44 g carbohydrates, 5 g fat, 2 mg cholesterol, 4 g fiber, 525 mg sodium*

# Peppery Cornbread

1   cup buttermilk
⅓   cup water
1   egg
3   tablespoons canola oil
3   tablespoons sugar
1¼ cups cornmeal
1   cup unbleached all-purpose flour
1¾ teaspoons baking powder
½   teaspoon baking soda
½   teaspoon salt
1½ teaspoons crushed red-pepper flakes

*Crushed red-pepper flakes give this all-American quick bread zing. Served hot, the pepper flavor is quite a bit stronger than when cooled before eating. Savor it with a creamy chowder.*

Preheat the oven to 425°F. Grease an 8" x 8" nonstick baking pan.

In a bowl, whisk together the buttermilk, water, egg, oil, and sugar.

In a large bowl, combine the cornmeal, flour, baking powder, baking soda, salt, and red-pepper flakes. Add the buttermilk mixture and stir just until a moistened batter forms.

Spread the batter into the prepared pan. Bake for 15 minutes, or until lightly browned and a wooden pick inserted in the center comes out clean. Let cool on a rack for 5 minutes before serving.

**Makes one 8" x 8" square loaf (9 squares)**
*Per serving: 198 calories, 5 g protein, 31 g carbohydrates, 7 g fat, 25 mg cholesterol, 2 g fiber, 501 mg sodium*

# Whole Wheat Bread

2 packages (¼ ounce each) active dry yeast

2½ cups warm water (105°–115°F)

¼ cup honey

2 teaspoons salt

1 tablespoon canola oil

3 cups whole wheat flour

1 tablespoon gluten (optional)

3½ cups bread flour

*This hearty, dense loaf is sweetened with honey to complement the wheat's nutlike flavor. Serve it with any hearty soup or stew.*

In a large mixing bowl, dissolve the yeast in the water. Stir in the honey and let stand for 5 minutes, or until the yeast is foamy. Stir in the salt, oil, 2 cups of the whole wheat flour, and the gluten, if using. Beat until smooth. Stir in the remaining whole wheat flour and enough of the bread flour to form a soft dough. Cover with a damp cloth and let rest for 15 minutes.

Turn out onto a lightly floured surface and knead for 10 minutes, or until the dough is smooth and elastic.

Coat a clean large bowl with cooking spray. Place the dough in the bowl, turn the dough, cover the bowl with a damp towel, and let rise in a warm place for 35 minutes, or until the dough is light and doubled in bulk.

Grease two 9" x 5" or 8" x 4" loaf pans. Gently deflate the dough with your fist and knead to eliminate air bubbles. Divide the dough into 2 equal-size pieces and shape into oblong loaves. Place in the prepared pans, cover with a damp cloth, and let rise in a warm place for 40 to 45 minutes, or until the dough is light and almost doubled in size.

Preheat the oven to 375°F. Bake the loaves for 30 minutes. Reduce the heat to 350°, and bake for 10 minutes longer, or until the crust is golden and the loaves sound hollow when tapped. Immediately remove from the pans and cool on a rack.

**Makes 32 servings**

*Per serving: 203 calories, 7 g protein, 42 g carbohydrates, 2 g fat, 0 mg cholesterol, 4 g fiber, 295 mg sodium*

# Index

**Boldface references indicate photographs.**

# CONVERSION CHART

These equivalents have been slightly rounded to make measuring easier.

### VOLUME MEASUREMENTS

| U.S. | Imperial | Metric |
|------|----------|--------|
| ¼ tsp | – | 1 ml |
| ½ tsp | – | 2 ml |
| 1 tsp | – | 5 ml |
| 1 Tbsp | – | 15 ml |
| 2 Tbsp (1 oz) | 1 fl oz | 30 ml |
| ¼ cup (2 oz) | 2 fl oz | 60 ml |
| ⅓ cup (3 oz) | 3 fl oz | 80 ml |
| ½ cup (4 oz) | 4 fl oz | 120 ml |
| ⅔ cup (5 oz) | 5 fl oz | 160 ml |
| ¾ cup (6 oz) | 6 fl oz | 180 ml |
| 1 cup (8 oz) | 8 fl oz | 240 ml |

### WEIGHT MEASUREMENTS

| U.S. | Metric |
|------|--------|
| 1 oz | 30 g |
| 2 oz | 60 g |
| 4 oz (¼ lb) | 115 g |
| 5 oz (⅓ lb) | 145 g |
| 6 oz | 170 g |
| 7 oz | 200 g |
| 8 oz (½ lb) | 230 g |
| 10 oz | 285 g |
| 12 oz (¾ lb) | 340 g |
| 14 oz | 400 g |
| 16 oz (1 lb) | 455 g |
| 2.2 lb | 1 kg |

### LENGTH MEASUREMENTS

| U.S. | Metric |
|------|--------|
| ¼" | 0.6 cm |
| ½" | 1.25 cm |
| 1" | 2.5 cm |
| 2" | 5 cm |
| 4" | 11 cm |
| 6" | 15 cm |
| 8" | 20 cm |
| 10" | 25 cm |
| 12" (1') | 30 cm |

### PAN SIZES

| U.S. | Metric |
|------|--------|
| 8" cake pan | 20 × 4 cm sandwich or cake tin |
| 9" cake pan | 23 × 3.5 cm sandwich or cake tin |
| 11" × 7" baking pan | 28 × 18 cm baking tin |
| 13" × 9" baking pan | 32.5 × 23 cm baking tin |
| 15" × 10" baking pan | 38 × 25.5 cm baking tin (Swiss roll tin) |
| 2 qt rectangular baking dish | 30 × 19 cm baking dish |
| 1½ qt baking dish | 1.5 liter baking dish |
| 2 qt baking dish | 2 liter baking dish |
| 9" pie plate | 22 × 4 or 23 × 4 cm pie plate |
| 7" or 8" springform pan | 18 or 20 cm springform or loose-bottom cake tin |
| 9" × 5" loaf pan | 23 × 13 cm or 2 lb narrow loaf tin or pâté tin |

### TEMPERATURES

| Fahrenheit | Centigrade | Gas |
|------------|------------|-----|
| 140° | 60° | – |
| 160° | 70° | – |
| 180° | 80° | – |
| 225° | 110° | – |
| 250° | 120° | ½ |
| 300° | 150° | 2 |
| 325° | 160° | 3 |
| 350° | 180° | 4 |
| 375° | 190° | 5 |
| 400° | 200° | 6 |
| 450° | 230° | 8 |
| 500° | 260° | – |